A BIBLIOGRAPHY
of
CROATIAN DICTIONARIES

BY THE SAME AUTHOR

La Langue littéraire croate, NEL, Paris 1972
L'Influence de la langue française en Croatie, NEL, Paris 1975
Det kroatiska litterära språket, Lund 1975
Les Mots d'emprunt français en croate, NEL, Paris 1976
An Historical Survey of Literary Croatian, NEL, Paris 1984

A BIBLIOGRAPHY
of
CROATIAN
DICTIONARIES

Branko Franolić
Docteur ès Lettres

NOUVELLES EDITIONS LATINES, PARIS

ISBN 2 7233 0302-0

Nouvelles Editions Latines, 1 Rue Palatine — 75006 Paris
Printed in Great Britain by
Whitstable Litho Ltd., Whitstable, Kent

FOREWORD

Dictionaries have played an important part in the evolution and growth of Standard Croatian and the need for a bibliography has long been felt. This *Bibliography of Croatian Dictionaries* is the first attempt to provide a comprehensive and up-to-date bibliography of dictionaries of Croatian. It does not claim to be free from error; no work of this kind can ensure this. Its modest aim is to help the user to find as much relevant information on Croatian lexicography as possible and to provide guidance for those seeking background information on Croatian dictionaries.

B. F.

AN HISTORICAL OUTLINE
OF CROATIAN LEXICOGRAPHY

The oldest Croatian interlinear or marginal glosses in manuscripts are preserved in the Radon Bible (Latin manuscript
from 8th-9th centuries, produced somewhere in the north of
France and now kept in Vienna). These glosses go back to 11th-
12th centuries and preserve the earliest recorded forms in
Croatian. It seems that they were written in Zagreb during the
episcopate of the first Zagreb bishop, Duh, who came from
Bohemia and was probably conversant with Glagolitic
literature. Besides Bohemianisms, these glosses also contain
many Croatian (Kajkavic) terms, such as *često, počivališće,
ot severa, vednunt, zetua*[1] (Hamm 1952). These glosses are
our earliest evidence of cultural ties with the oldest Western
lexicographical works, the *Reichenau glosses*, 8th century
manuscripts containing a set of French glosses to the Vulgate
Bible of St. Jerome and the *Kassel glosses* from the early 9th
century. Croatian glosses are also to be found in Zagreb medi-
aeval Latin codices, especially in school manuals. One could
also mention Croatian Kajkavic glosses from the 16th century
contained in Joannes Balbus's *Catholicon* in the Pauline
monastery at Remete near Zagreb.

The first lexicographical attempts in Croatia and among
Croats began during the period of Humanism and Renaissance.
With the rise of vernacular languages during the Renaissance,
translating into and from Latin had great importance. Since
Latin was a language of great prestige well into modern times,
Latin dictionaries were very important in the later development
of European lexicography and interlingual or polyglot dictionaries incorporating Latin developed early. The major lexicographical work of this period, preserved in manuscript, is a
sizeable polyglot Arabic-Greek-Latin-Croatian dictionary of
botanical and pharmacological terms, *Liber de Simplicibus*.
This specialized encyclopedic dictionary, explaining concepts

as well as words, was compiled in Zadar (ca. 1445) by the physician Niccolò Roccabonella (Minio 1953). The codex is kept in Marciana Library in Venice. As every entry is illustrated by a picture of a plant, it is also the first Croatian pictorial dictionary, containing 432 beautiful pictures. The pictures of the plants were apparently painted by the quattrocento Miniaturist from Zadar. The English author and art critic John Ruskin (1819-1900) was so enchanted by the pictorial beauty of the codex that he had the pictures copied for him by the Venetian painter Caldara (De Toni 1925 : 179).

About 1496-99 Arnold von Harff from Köln (Cologne) recorded some 56 Croat words on his journey through Croatia. This 'corpus' (of words) remained unpublished till 1860, when von Harff's book of travels was finally edited by E. Groote (Pajk 1889).

Two other 15th century dictionaries are also preserved in manuscript, one of which is a trilingual Arabic-Persian-Croatian dictionary (Rešetar 1904).

The first printed list of Croatian words is actually to be found in *Opera nuova che insegna a parlare la lingua schiavonesca alli grandi, alli picoli et alle donne* published in 1527, in all likelihood in Ancona. This work contains a small Italian-Croat glossary of 196 Italian lexical items and 328 Croatian terms with some conversational texts and a model of a letter. Its author is probably the Spanish Jew, Pietro Lupis (López) Valentiano, who fled from Spain in 1492 and afterwards settled in Ancona (Italy) as a merchant. From Italy he traded with Dalmatia and came into close contact with people living in the towns along the Croat littoral. This is why he uses chiefly the Čakavic *i*-dialect in the Croat part of his work, the original of which is preserved in Bayerische Staatsbibliothek in Munich (Petr 1973, Putanec 1979[a]).

Ten years later *Lexicum Symphonum* was published in Basle (1537). This comparative dictionary of four languages (*graece, latine, germanice ac sclavinice*) includes a certain number of Croatian words. It was compiled by the Czech Humanist Sigismund Gelenius (Hrubý) who met Croatian students and scholars (Julius Camillus) while studying in Italy and

Germany and probably learnt some Croatian from them. *Lexicum Symphonum* contains over 500 Czech and a few Croatian words, 560 (Czech and Croatian) terms altogether but, because of the similarity between the two languages, it is difficult to identify the Croatian words with certainty (Schmaus 1956).

Some Croatian terms are also included in *Knížka slov českých* (Prague 1587), a Czech dictionary with purist tendencies and etymological pretensions, compiled by Matouš Beneškovski (Philonomus).

Seventeen years after the publication of *Opera nuova* Bartholomaeus Đurđević (Georgević) had the insight to supplement his Latin work, *De Afflictione tam captivorum quam etiam sub Turcae tributo viventium Christianorum* (Antwerp 1544, in-8°), with a systematic, analytical Croat-Latin vocabulary (*Vocabula Sclavonica*, 52 words and phrases), preceded by a brief dialogue in Croatian with an interlinear Latin translation. *Vocabula Sclavonica* are grouped analytically under five headings: *Coelestia* (12), *Terrena* (19), *Fructum* (8), 'verbal phrases' (8), *Nomina vestimentorum* (5). Edited in one volume, *De Afflictione* contains also French, Dutch and English versions of the Latin text. Consequently we also have here the first interlingual Croat-French, Croat-Dutch and Croat-English vocabularies. This volume also contains *Dominica Oratio* (the Lord's Prayer), *Salutatio Angelica* (Hail Mary) and *Symbolum Apostolorum* (the Apostles' Creed) in Čakavic; and Croatian numerals from one to one hundred and one thousand with their equivalents in Latin, French, Dutch and English. The Croatian numerals were also recorded by the Italian cinquecentist, Angelo Rocca (1545-1620), the bishop of Tagaste (Marche) who in the 16th century published a collection of *Pater noster* in many languages and Italian dialects, including many topics of linguistic concern (Cartelazzo 1980 : 68). On page 321 of his *Opera Omnia, tomus secundus* (Rome 1719, in -4°), after *Modus Numerandi Illyrice*,[2] Rocca writes, *"Qui plura de Illyricà, & Polonicà lingua, scitu quidem digna, noscere cupit, Bartholomaei scripta, & Gelenii, qui de ea copiose scripserunt per legere studeat. Haec hactenus,"* which clearly indicates that Rocca knew the works of Bartholomeus Đurđević and Gelenius.

The Croat dialect used by Đurđević is Čakavic *i*-dialect which proves conclusively that Đurđević was born in the Čakavic speaking area of Croatia (Baudouin de Courtenay 1888). More precisely, he was born in Mala Mlaka ca. 1506 and died in Rome 1566. He was taken prisoner by the Turks at the battle of Mohács in 1526, and spent nine years as a slave, mostly in Asia Minor where he learned Turkish. After escaping from Turkish captivity he devoted his life to writing popular works in Latin about the Turks. As these works were translated into Italian, French, German, English, Dutch, Polish and Czech, no Croatian Humanist was so widely read throughout all of Europe in his day as Bartol Đurđević (Kidrič 1920).

Another wandering Humanist and polyhistor, Paul Skalić (Zagreb 1534—Gdańsk 1573), published his work, *Encyclopaedia seu orbis disciplinarum tam sacrarum quam prophanarum epistemon* (Encyclopaedia, or Knowledge of the World of Disciplines. . .), in Basle in 1559. Although it is not a dictionary properly speaking but a publication containing 'a more heterogeneous collection of essays' (*Encyclopedia Britannica* (1971) Vol. 8, 363), it is worth mentioning here since it is "the first work known to contain the word [encyclopedia] in the title" (cf. *The Encyclopedia Americana* (1979), Vol. 10, 330). "Scalich's Encyclopaedia brought the term back into prominence." (*The Macmillan Family Encyclopedia*, Vol. 7, p. 163). By the same token, in the second decade of the 16th century, the Humanist Marko Marulić (1450-1524) from Split was the author of the first work in Europe to be entitled Psychology: *Psychologia de ratione animae humanae lib 1*, probably written between 1511 and 1518 (Lapointe 1972, Brozek 1973).

Between 1537 and 1595 an Italian-Croatian glossary was also compiled which is now preserved in the Bodleian Library at Oxford (MS, *Selden Supra* 95). It contains 1716 Italian lexical items (: words, short syntagmas, e.g. *bono sacerdote*, and short phrases, e.g. *andiamo insino alla chiesa*) with Croatian (West Čakavic) equivalents. There are to be found approximately 1800 lexemes for each language since some lexical items are explained by synonyms (Pohl 1976).

Croatian lexical material also appears in the alphabetical register appended to Pergošić's *Decretum* (1574), a translation of Verböczy's *Tripartitum opus Juris Consuetudinarii Regni Hungariae* (1517), in the differential Slovenian-Croatian dictionaries added to *the Pentateuch* (Ljubljana 1578) and to *the Bible* (Wittenberg 1584), translated into Slovenian by the Protestant writer Juraj Dalmatin (1547-89). These differential Slovenian-Croatian glossaries grew out of the desire of Juraj Dalmatin and South-Slav supporters of the Reformation that Croatians and 'other Slovenians' should be able to understand the Scriptures in their own vernaculars. The register of *the Pentateuch* contains 206 Slovenian lexical items and 345 Croatian words, while that of *the Bible* contains 761 Slovenian items and 998 Croatian words (Putanec 1979[b]). Translations of the bible indirectly produced powerful aids to establishing equivalents of Latin and Greek words and expressions in modern languages.

Another Protestant Humanist, the German polyhistor Hieronimus Megiser (1554-1619) of Stuttgart, in his *Dictionarium quatuor linguarum videlicet Germanicae, Latinae, Illyricae (quae vulgo Sclavonica appelatur) et Italicae sive Hetruscae* (Graz 1592, Frankfurt 1608, Klagenfurt 1744) and later in his *Thesaurus polyglottus* (1603), included many Slovenian and Croatian words. Megiser spent some time in the city of Rijeka and in Istria and many Croatian words recorded in his dictionaries are taken from the Čakavic dialect spoken in that area.

In 1595 the *Dictionarium Quinque Nobilissimarum Europae Linguarum, Latinae, Italicae, Germanicae, Dalmatiae et Ungaricae Fausti Verantii* was published in Venice *apud Nicolaum Morettum* (VI + 128 in -8°). This multilingual dictionary is often regarded as the first major dictionary of the Croatian language and its author, Faust Vrančić (1551-1617), as the father of Croatian lexicography. Vrančić's work undoubtedly represents a major landmark in the history of Croatian and indeed European lexicography.

Vrančić's Dictionary is a fairly slim volume but it is packed with lexical material. On each page, in five columns, lexical equivalents of the same terms are given in five different languages. The first column contains Latin words, the second Italian, the third German, the fourth Croatian and the fifth Hungarian. The basic assumption underlying such an effort is that there exist certain syntactic and semantic invariants which make lingustic comparisons of this nature both possible and fruitful.

Altogether over five thousand lexical units are recorded by Vrančić in each of the five languages, side by side. Substantives of inflected languages are given in nominative form and verbs in the infinitive. Vrančić's Croatian is based on the Čakavic dialect of his native Dalmatia where Čakavic Croatian is still spoken today. Incidentally the oldest Croatian literary language was based on the Čakavic dialect and it was in the 16th century that the literature written in this dialect had its 'golden season', with intense literary activity flourishing in all the major Adriatic towns of Southern Croatia, from Senj to Kotor. As Vrančić was born in Šibenik in Dalmatia, Čakavic was naturally the dialect he knew and remembered best during his long years abroad. In fact he spent most of his life outside his native country: in Vienna, Venice, Rome and in various places in Hungary.

It is interesting to note that on pages 118-122 of the Dictionary, Vrančić lists 304 Hungarian words which he regards as being of Croatian origin (*Vocabula Dalmatica que Ungari sibi usurparunt*). Consequently this Dictionary must also be regarded as one of the first attempts to study the etymology of borrowings from one language to another resulting—as in this case—from a prolonged linguistic contact. At this point one ought to recall that in 1102 Croatia entered into a political union with the Kingdom of Hungary which lasted seven centuries. The union was based on a treaty (*Pacta Conventa*) whereby the Croats, following a military defeat at the hands of the Hungarians, agreed to accept the Hungarian King but retained a considerable measure of internal autonomy. This accounts for the fact that when Vrančić was compiling his

Dictionary there was quite a large number of Croatian loan-words in Hungarian, and vice versa.

Vrančić obviously knew Hungarian extremely well and it is certainly interesting that his Dictionary was also the first major lexicon of the Hungarian language. He probably learned Hungarian when he was still a young man, for he was partly educated and helped by his uncle Antun Vrančić (1504-1573), a distinguished clergyman and scholar who spent most of his life in Hungary. Antun died in 1573 as Emperor Maximilian's Regent in Hungary, Primate of Hungary and a cardinal. Faust Vrančić himself took holy orders after his wife's death in 1600 and became Bishop of the Hungarian diocese of Csanád.

Analysing the lexical material of Vrančić's Dictionary, with special reference to Hungarian, the eminent lexicologist Janos Melich rightly observes that Vrančić's Dictionary 'in every respect represents an independent and original work which does great credit to the history of both Hungarian and Croatian lexicography' (1906:36). Melich also thinks that Vrančić compiled his Dictionary before 1586, that is, while Stephen Báthory, King of Poland between 1575-86, was still alive. Because of its great importance to Hungarian lexicology, Vrančić's Dictionary was republished in 1834 in Bratislava by the Hungarian scholar Joseph Thewrewk under the title *Dictionarium pentaglottum*, with a biography of Vrančić written by Georgius Gyurikovits.

Vrančić's Dictionary stimulated similar efforts by other lexicographers. Thus his Dictionary was used by the Czech Benedictine monk Peter Loderecker as a basis for his own *Dictionarium septem diversarum linguarum, videlicet Latine, Italice, Dalmatice, Bohemice, Polonice, Germanice et Ungarice*, published in Prague in 1605. This dictionary contains a preface in Croatian written by Faust Vrančić himself. In fact Loderecker's Dictionary was essentially Vrančić's own *Dictionarium quinque nobilissimarum Europae linguarum* of 1595, revised and expanded by Loderecker to include Czech and Polish with added indices in Latin for each language. In this Loderecker-Vrančić Dictionary the terms *Dalmata, Dalmatia, Dalmatice* are explained as *Harvat* (Croat), *Harvatska zemlja*

13

(Croatia), *Harvatski* (Croatian), which entitles us, not only from a linguistic but also from an historical point of view, to refer to 'lingua dalmatica' of this Dictionary as 'Croatian'; 'Dalmatian' being a geographical and not an ethnic designation, although, given Croatia's political plight at the time, probably better known abroad, where Vrančić lived.

There is another important detail which should be mentioned when discussing the significance of Vrančić's Dictionary in the history of the Croatian language: namely, that in the last six pages of his book Vrančić recorded the complete Croatian text of the Ten Commandments, the Lord's Prayer, the Apostles' Creed and Ave Maria. These are invaluable samples of the 16th century Croatian vernacular spoken in Dalmatia at the time.

It is only recently, in an elaborate study, that the Croat terms recorded in the dictionary have been examined in detail, with reference to the place and time in which the dictionary was compiled (Putanec 1971). The Register of Croat-Latin lexical equivalents contained in Vrančić's dictionary is provided by V. Putanec in the 1971 reprint edition. This Register is an inventory of all the different Croat words which are to be found in Vrančić's dictionary and the frequency of every (Croat) word is also indicated. Vrančić's dictionary contains 5467 Latin lexical items, while in Putanec's Croat-Latin register there are 3581 Croat words.

"In assessing Vrančić's Dictionary one has to take into account the time when Vrančić was active. For the Croatian literary language this was the period of many unsettled problems: the Croatian version of Old Slavonic was coming to an end. Glagolitic script was in decline and the Latin script was not yet fully mastered. In those days every author was a potential reformer. This difficult task was assumed also by Faust Vrančić. In defining the geographical area covered by the language "from the Adriatic to the Drava and the Danube rivers", he remained faithful to the tradition of exposing Čakavic to other dialects (including Kajkavic and especially Štokavic). In the matter of orthography he attempted to overcome discrepancies between the use of the Latin script in the south and the north, thus making way for the implementation of a Latin script which would be based on the phonetic and phonological requirements of the Croatian language." (Vončina 1979).

Faust Vrančić is renowned in the international world of learning as the author of *Machinae novae*, Venice 1595. He will also be remembered for his philosophical works *Logica nova*, Venice 1616, and *Ethica christiana* (Dictionary of Scientific Biography 1976 : XIII, 613-614).

It is worth noting that the 17th century *Vocabularium trilingue* (Croatian-Italian-Latin) preserved in manuscript in Perugia, was largely based on Vrančić's dictionary. The author of this work, an anonymus compiler, probably an Italian from Dalmatia, made free use of the work of earlier compilers, as was the custom of the time.

In 1606, the Frenchman, Jean Palerne, had his *Pérégrinations*, a travelogue describing his journey to the Levant between 1581-83, published in Lyons. To this travelogue was annexed a small dictionary 'en langue françois, Italien, Grec vulgaire, Turc, Moresque ou Arabesque et Esclavon'. It is an analytical, systematic dictionary followed by the most common conversational dialogues. On his way to the Levant, Palerne visited Dalmatia (Dubrovnik) and the Croatian words recorded in his dictionary are taken from the *što -ije* dialect of Dubrovnik.

In the first half of the 17th century, Hevājī Uskúfī, a Muslim from Tuzla (Bosnia), compiled a small Croatian-Turkish dictionary written in verses, completing it in 1631. It is known under the name of *Potur-Šāhìdī* although its original colourful title is *Makbûli-'arif* (What is pleasing to the reasonable ones). Alija Nametak published an annotated edition of this dictionary in 1968 (Nametak 1968, 1978).

Vocabulario Nouvo — Zvanik Novii (Italian-Croatian Dictionary) was also written in the first half of the 17th century and published in 1655. It is a conversational lexicographic manual designed for Italians wishing to learn Croatian and for Croats wishing to learn Italian. This booklet of 24 pages was reissued in Venice in 1703 and 1737 by the printer Bartolo Occhi and later in 1804. However, only a 1737 copy has been preserved in the library of the Franciscan monastery at Zaostrog. The Croatian term *zvanik* which figures in the subtitle of the manual is a linguistic calque of the Italian word *vocabulario* (cf. Latin *vocare* = Cr. *zvati*) (Putanec 1979[c], Kosor 1975, Galić 1981).

Many literary men of that time felt the inadequacy of Croatian dictionaries, particularly in view of the Italian examples. Thus the first interlingual dictionaries with Croatian entries in alphabetical order appeared between 1650 and 1670. *Blago jezika slovinskoga* (*Thesaurus of the Croatian language*) (Loreto-Ancona 1649-1651), compiled by the Jesuit Jakob Mikalja (1601-1654), contains Latin and Italian lexical equivalents of approximately 25000 Croatian words taken from *što -je-* and *ča -i-* dialects. It also contains a number of locutions or phrases then in current use and is five times bigger than Vrančić's *Dictionarium*. Mikalja's dictionary is of considerable interest to the history of Croatian and was much drawn upon by later lexicographers. Mikalja intended his dictionary "for the children of Dalmatia" and was more concerned with producing a practical aid to communication than philological interest in classification and analysis of words and their relationships, although he recorded a great number of synonyms and variants used in different (*što* and *ča*) dialects with many cross-references. In the preface to his dictionary Mikalja wrote that *"La lingua bosnese* (i. e. *što*-dialect) *sia la più bella"*, and he thought that this Štokavic dialect could be compared with the Central Italian dialects of Tuscany which form the backbone of the literary Italian language. The term *blago*, contained in the title, is a Croatian equivalent of the Greek word *thesaurus* which in Latin acquired the figurative sense "store-house of knowledge", and during the Renaissance it became the title of several great dictionaries of Greek and Latin.

Slightly smaller than Mikalja's work is *Dikcionar, ili Reči slovenske zvekšega vkup zebrane* (Graz 1670), a Croatian (Kajkavic)-Latin dictionary, compiled by the Jesuit Juraj Habdelič (1609-78). It is the first Croatian Kajkavic dictionary containing about 10,000 Croatian words. Habdelič was a school teacher in Zagreb and the writer of some significance. His collections of sermons (*The Mirror of Mary* and *The Original Sin of our Father Adam*) are written in excellent Croatian and contain many valuable and exact observations of life around him.

Several other dictionaries were compiled in the 17th century, such as Grgur de Vitalibus's *Dictionarium trium nobilissimarum Europae linguarum, latinae, illyricae et italicae* (Romae 1628), in two volumes, which, to our knowledge, has not been preserved. Conversely, Tanzlinger-Zanotti's *Vocabolario di tre nobilissimi linguaggi, italiano, illirico e latino* (in three redactions: 1679[1], 138 leaves in folio, 1704[2], 1281 pp, 1732[3]) and *Slovoslovlje*, a bilingual Croatian (Čakavic)-Italian dictionary, have been preserved in manuscript in several copies.

Vitezović's *Lexicon latino-illyricum*, 1132 pages in -4°, compiled at the beginning of the 18th century (1700-1709), has also been preserved in the archbishopric library in Zagreb (The Bibliotheca Metropolitana MR. 112). This dictionary contains the words of the three basic dialects and many Bohemianisms. Pavao Ritter Vitezović (1652-1712) was neither a nobleman nor a cleric but the first Croatian who tried to live from his writing and publishing activities. He was a prolific and versatile intellectual whose concern extended to linguistics and orthography.

In the first half of the 18th century, three encyclopedic dictionaries were published: Ardelio della Bella's *Dizionario italiano-latino-illirico* (Venezia, 1728; 2 ed: Dubrovnik, 1785, 2 vol.), Ivan Belostenec's *Gazophylacium seu latino-illyricorum onomatum aerarium* (Zagreb, 1740) and Andrija Jambrešić's *Lexicon latinum interpretatione Illyrica, Germanica et Hungarica locuples* (Zagreb, 1742).

Belostenec's *Gazophylacium* has two parts: *Latino-illyricum* (14 + 1288 pp. containing about 40,000 Latin words) and *Illyrico-latinum* (650 + 42 pp. containing about 25,000 Croatian words). Besides lexical items, it contains a great number of locutions or phrases, metaphors and gnomic expressions (proverbs, sayings, etc.). It includes the words of the three basic Croatian dialects: Kajkavic words from the region of Karlovac, Čakavic from Croatian Littoral and Istria and Što-kavic words used in Slavonia and Dalmatia. It is obvious that Belostenec was familiar with Vrančić's *Dictionarium Quinque Nobilissimarum Europae Linguarum* (1595) and was also able to use Mikalja's *Blago jezika slovinskoga* (1649-51). He also largely drew upon Habdelič's *Dikcionar* while compiling the second part (illyrico-latinum) of his *Gazophylacium*, which he never completed since he died in 1675. After Belostenec's death *Gazophylacium* was slightly enlarged and revised by Jeronim Orlović and finally published in 1740. This explains why the influence of Della Bella's *Dizionario*, published in 1728, is to be seen in it.

Sharing the view of the Catholic writer Franjo Glavinić (1586-1650) and the 16th century Protestant writers, that the words of the three main dialects must all be included in the Croatian lexicon (word-stock), Belostenec greatly influenced the later development of the Croatian literary language by incorporating the so-called dialect contact synonyms into his *Gazophylacium* (e.g. Lat. *vinea* = Cr. *tersje, vinograd*; Lat. *silva* = Cr. *loza, gaj,* etc.). Belostenec's dictionary rightly had enormous influence and its publication was the most important linguistic event of the eighteenth century.

Because of its importance to the history of the Croatian literary language, the reprint edition of *Gazophylacium* was published in 1973 by Zagreb University Press *Liber*. Belo-stenec's dictionary cannot be properly evaluated unless it is seen in a wider historical context (Vončina 1973). As *Liber's* Editor wrote in his address at the end of the 1973 reprint edition: "Italian was the first among the living European languages to get a comprehensive encyclopaedic dictionary. This dictionary was published in 1612. (The Accademia della Crusca of Florence, brought out its *Vocabolario* in Venice in 1612). The next similar dictionary was the great dictionary of the French Academy which appeared 82 years later—in 1694. (Two other French dictionaries were actually more scholarly—that of César-Pierre Richelet in 1680 and that of Antoine Fouretière in 1690). Somewhere between these two dates, on the very edge of the Europe of that time, only 30 kilometres or so away from the ever restless Turkish frontier, the Pauline Prior Ivan Belostenec . . . devoted his life to his *Gazophylacium.''* Academies of scholars had taken decades to compile the standard French and Italian dictionaries. Belostenec set out to supply single-handed the equivalent for Croatian.

The Italian Jesuit Ardelio Della Bella (1655-1737), who had lived for a long time in Dubrovnik and in other parts of Dalmatia, had his trilingual *Dizionario Italiano-Latino-Illirico* (50 + 785 + 177 pp.) published in Venice in 1728. Using as a model the Italian dictionary (*Vocabolario*) published in Venice in 1612 by the Accademia della Crusca of Florence[3], Della Bella was the first to fill his *Dizionario* with copious quotations (4000-5000) from Croatian literature. Besides quotations from literature in *što -ije* language (Dubrovnik), the *Dizionario* includes many Čakavic words taken from the works of the writers (Petar Hektorović, Hanibal Lucić) who wrote in *ča*-language. When he attempted to codify the Croatian language in his dictionary Della Bella selected the written forms of Croatian which enjoyed social prestige.

The first edition of the *Dizionario* also contains a Latin-Italian index of words (177 pp.). The second edition, revised and enlarged by Petar Bašić (1749-1814), was brought out in 1785 in two volumes (Vol. I, A-H LVI + 395 pp. Vol. II, 448 pp.). The second edition also incorporates many phrases, proverbs and some coinages or neologies. Both editions contain a Croatian grammar written in Italian. As some words in this dictionary have prosodic marks (suprasegmental graphemes) written above them, it may also serve as a source for the historical study of accentuation in Croatian.

Lexicon latinum interpretatione Illyrica, Germanica et Hungarica locuples (Zagreb 1742) was compiled by two Jesuits. It was started by Franjo Sušnik (1686-1739) and completed by Andrija Jambrešić (1706-58). It contains two parts: the first part is a Latin-Croatian-German-Hungarian dictionary (1068 pages containing about 27,000 Latin words), the second is a Croatian-Latin index (*Index Illyrico sive Croatico-Latinus*) for ease of reference (92 pages containing about 7000 Croatian words). The Croatian words incorporated in the dictionary are mainly Kajkavic but there are also many Štokavic and Čakavic words or contact synonyms. It is a very independent and original work as Jambrešić did not draw upon or glean from the dictionaries of previous lexicographers: Vrančić, Mikalja or Della Bella. The information about the lexical items in the dictionary is scantier than in *Gazophylacium* but their semantic definition is more accurate (Dukat 1905).

It is worth noting that Jambrešić also brought out *Manuductio ad croaticam orthographiam* (Manual of Croatian Orthography, Zagreb, 1732) in which he proposed the reform of Croatian Latin script and the introduction of the diacritics *č*, *š* and *ž*, as in Czech, a century before Ljudevit Gaj, the 19th century reformer of Croatian spelling and orthography. His dictionary also contains some suggestions for the reform of Croatian orthography.

Apart from these standard dictionaries, fourteen other lexicographic works were compiled in the 18th century. Four were printed, ten remained in manuscript. Among the ten unpublished dictionaries three are worth mentioning: the Kajkavic *Dictionarium latino-illyricum et germanicum* (1054 pp.) by Adam Patačić (1716-84). It is a compendium of philosophy and general knowledge lexicon, written between 1772 and 1779 and designed for young students. *Nomenclator omnium rerum propria nomina variis linguis explicata continens* brought out by the Dutch Humanist, Hadrianus Junius, in 1567 served to Patačić as a model regarding the composition of his dictionary and the classification of different subject matters. The manuscript of Patačić's dictionary is preserved in the archbishop's library in Kalocza (Hungary) where Patačić died as archbishop (Jonke 1949).

The Franciscan Josip Jurin (1730-1802) compiled a large trilingual dictionary, *Calepinus trium linguarum*, in three parts (Part I: Latin-Croatian-Italian, Part II: Italian-Latin-Croatian, Part III: an alphabetical list of contributions). The Croatian words in this unpublished dictionary belong to Štokavic and Čakavic dialects and it contains more botanical, ichthyological and ornithological terms than the dictionaries of Mikalja and Della Bella.

The third unpublished dictionary, *Etymologicon Illyricum* (*Pravoslovnik*, 1473 pp.), was compiled by the Franciscan polyhistor and poet, Matija Petar Katančić (1751-1825). *Pravoslovnik* is a calque of *etymologicon* (Greek *etymos* = Cr. *pravi*; -*slovnik* 'dictionary, word-book' stands for -*logicon*]. It is an etymological dictionary which lacks precision concerning the origin and history of words and is full of etymological fallacies. The manuscript of this dictionary, containing 53,000 lexical items, up to the last entry *svemoguć* is preserved in Budapest University library.

Of the four printed lexicographical works, two are Latin-Croatian (Kajkavic) phraseological dictionaries: Ivan Galjuf's Croatian version of François Pomey's *Flos latinitatis* (Zagreb, 1747, 1797², 1820³, 1834⁴) and F. Wagner's *Syntaxis ornata* (Zagreb, 1747). Two others are a trilingual *Radices linguae Latinae cum derivatis suis in tribus idiomatibus Latino-Croatico-Germanico* (Zagreb, 1788; Buda, 1801) and a bilingual German-Croatian conversational dictionary *Svašta po malo* (A Little of Everything, Magdeburg, 1761) compiled by Blaž Tadijanović.

At the very beginning of the 19th century two trilingual dictionaries were printed. Both are imbued with the pre-romantic and pan-Slavic concepts of a common ethnic and linguistic origin of the various Slav peoples. Joakim Stulli's dictionary, although completed in 1782, was published only many years later in three separate parts (six thick volumes). The first part, *Lexicon latino-italico-illyricum* (1620 pp in -4°), was published in Budapest in 1801; the second, *Rječjosložje slovinsko-italijansko-latinsko* (1401 pp.), was printed in Dubrovnik in 1806, and the third, *Vocabolario italiano-illirico-latino* (1700 pp.), was also published in Dubrovnik in 1810. This encyclopedic dictionary has 4721 pages: while the second part alone contains a greater number of Croatian words than ever before appeared in any similar dictionary, 80,000 lexical items. The majority of Croatian words entered in the dictionary belong to the *što -ije* dialect but there are also some Čakavic and Kajkavic terms.

In the preface to his Lexicon (1801) Stulli writes: *"Itaque quodquod Illyri qualibet dialecto utantur, his suas voces reperient"*, that is to say that in his Lexicon the words of all Illyrian (Croatian) dialects are recorded, while the entry *illyrice*, in the Lexicon, is explained as *slovinski, Hârvatski, hrovatski, horvatski...*

In his dictionary Stulli (1730-1817) recorded words peculiar to the popular, peasant vernacular, but the majority of recorded words was taken from literary works, printed books and old manuscripts. He also drew upon the works of previous lexicographers (Mikalja, Habdelić, Della Bella, Belostenec and Jambrešić) and filled his dictionary with copious, illustrative quotations from Croatian literature, from the works of one hundred and twenty different writers. Besides many derivatives and neologisms coined by himself, Stulli entered in his dictionary many Russian, Polish and Czech words—thus demonstrating similarity among Slavonic languages and trying to stimulate "Slavic mutuality", that is a broad give-and-take among Slavic languages. Compiling Latin and Italian lexical material for his dictionary, Stulli drew profusely upon *'Taurinens Lexicon'*, an Italian-Latin and Latin-Italian dictionary, known as *Vocabolario di Torino*. Stulli's dictionary influenced the development of written and spoken Croatian in the first half of the 19th century, especially in Dalmatia. It was also a major source for the later lexicographers: Bogoslav Šulek, Ivan Broz and Franjo Iveković. Stulli's influence on Croat lexicography and literature was considerable. He laid the groundwork on which the *Dictionary of the Yugoslav Academy* (1881-1976) is based. Vladimir Mažuranić in his *Contributions to Croatian Legal and Historical Dictionary* (Zagreb, 1908-1922) refers to Stulli 900 times. P. Skok's *Etymological Dictionary* (Zagreb 1971-1974) refers to Stulli 1200 times and R. Simeon's *Encyclopedic Dictionary of Linguistic Terminology* (Zagreb 1969) refers to Stulli 500 times. It is worth noting that A. Jal's *Glossaire nautique — Répertoire polyglotte des termes de marine anciens et modernes* (Paris

1848-1850, 1591 pp.) contains a few hundred Croatian nautical terms taken from Stulli's Dictionary (Luetić 1956; Brlek 1980).

Another trilingual Croatian-Italian-German dictionary, *Ričoslovnik iliričkoga, italijanskoga i nimačkoga jezika* (Wien 1803, LIX+610 pp.), compiled by Josip Voltić (Voltiggi) (1750-1825), contains 17,000 words. The majority of Croatian entries in this dictionary belong to Čakavic dialect but it also contains many Štokavic and Kajkavic terms. Voltić drew upon the works of Mikalja, Della Bella, Belostenec and Stulli's Lexicon. This dictionary also lists many words pertaining to other Slavic languages. Yet while explaining the Croatian entries with Italian and German lexical and semantic equivalents, Voltić lacked lexicological accuracy.

Voltić's dictionary was designed as a school handbook intended for practical use. The need for such interlingual dictionaries intended for practical use was badly felt in Croatia at the beginning of the 19th century. To fill a need for such manuals, six small bilingual German-Croatian and Croatian-German dictionaries appeared in the first half of the 19th century. These were: (1) *Rječnik\ mali, das kleine Wörterbuch* (Budapest, 1806); (2) *Sprachübungen in der deutschen und kroatischen Sprache nebst einem deutsch-kroatischen Wörterbuch* (Karlovac 1823); (3) *Kleines kroatisches-deutsches Wörterbuch für die Jugend* (Zagreb 1829); (4) *Vocabularium croatico-germanicum, to jest nemške škole navuk kak Horvatom tak Nemcem na hasan* (Pečuh, 1925; 1841); (5) *Zbirka nekojih riječi* (Zagreb 1835, reprint from literary periodical *Danica*); (6) L. Škrobot, *Kleines illyrisch-deutsches Wörterbuch* (Zagreb 1839).

Apart from these minor dictionaries, the major Croatian-German and German-Croatian dictionary (*Ilirsko-njemački i njemačko-ilirski rukoslovnik*) compiled by M.A. Richter and A. Ballmann came out in Vienna in 1839-40. This dictionary was enlarged and revised by R.A. Veselić-Fröhlich and published under the title *Rječnik ilirskoga i njemačkoga jezika* (Wien 1853 and 1854). Slightly better is J. Drobnić's trilingual dictionary *Mali ilirsko-njemačko-talijanski rječnik* (Croatian-German-Italian) published in Vienna in 1846-49. However, the best bilingual dictionary of that period is *Njemačko-ilirski slovar* (German-Croatian dictionary) (Zagreb 1842) compiled by Ivan Mažuranić and Jakov Užarević. These dictionaries played an important part in the building of Modern Croatian lexicon. In a similar manner the lexicographical work *Juridisch-politische Terminologie für die slavischen Sprachen Österreichs (Deutsch-kroatische, serbische und slovenische Separat-Ausgabe)* was of great consequence to the formation of Croatian legal and political terminology. This last was published in Vienna in 1853.

In the second part of the 19th century many more interlingual dictionaries came out, those of the lexicographer Bogoslav Šulek (1816-1895), the founder of Croatian scientific terminology and modern lexicography, being prominent. Šulek's German-Croatian dictionary (*Deutsch-Kroatisches Wörterbuch*, Zagreb 1854-60, 2 vols. VIII, +1712 pp.) played a great part in fixing linguistic norms of standard Croatian. Šulek also compiled a specialised Croatian-German-Italian Dictionary of Scientific Terminology (*Rječnik znanstvenog nazivlja*, Zagreb, 1874-75, 2 vols. XXVI+1,372 pp.) which in reality was the joint enterprise of such Zagreb philologists as Vatroslav Jagić, Josip Torbar, Bogoslav Šulek, Franjo Erjavec, etc. This dictionary also contains a great number of French and English scientific and technical lexical equivalents. The dictionary had the normative aims of standardizing the scientific terminology in Croatia where the language had not yet been accommodated to modern technological needs. It was supplemented by the Dictionary of German-Croatian Technological Terminology (*Rječnik njemačko-hrvatskoga tehnologičkoga nazivlja*, Zagreb, 1881, 413 pp.). This first Croat Technological dictionary, containing 25,000 terms, was compiled and edited by the Club of Engineers and Architects.

In 1868 Ivan Dežman's Dictionary of Medical Terminology (*Rječnik liječničkog nazivlja*) was brought out and in 1879 Šulek's Yugoslav Botanical Nomenclature (*Jugoslavenski imenik bilja*, Zagreb, 1879, XXII+564 pp.), a major botanical lexicon, was also published.

Thus the necessary conditions for the development of

literary and learned Croatian were all satisfied at the time of the foundation of the South-Slav Academy in 1866 and the University of Zagreb in 1874. These two institutions stimulated a Croatian cultural revival which looked to Prague, Vienna and the West for inspiration. In his lexicographic works, Šulek and his collaborators adopted many words from both *kaj* and *ča* dialects. They also introduced into the written language a number of cultural borrowings, Bohemianisms and Russianisms as well as neologisms, thereby enabling the popular language to meet the needs of both literature and science. The new terms and turns of phrase introduced by Šulek have made it possible to express all the ideas resulting from the progress of science and the transformations of social life as well as new high-level concepts. Šulek also revived many words from the older language, notably the words recorded by the 17th and 18th century lexicographers.

However, while Šulek's vocabulary was not to be accepted in full, its penetration into the written Croatian language was so deep that even today the importance of his contribution is still recognised. The subsequent development of the Croatian litarary language has shown that it is impossible to do without a number of words introduced by Šulek. Šulek is also largely responsible for the creation of Croatian military terminology. From 1870 onwards he translated from Hungarian into Croat twenty booklets dealing with army life and military terminology. In 1953 the renowned linguist Petar Skok described the lexicographer Šulek as a linguistic genius, noting especially his skill in creating neologisms from resources within the language.

The importance of Dragutin Parčić's Croatian-Italian Dictionary (Zadar 1858[1] XIV+847 pp., 1874[2] VIII+1,059 pp., 1901[3] XII+1,237 pp.) and Italian-Croatian Dictionary (Zadar, 1868[1] 1,146 pp., Senj 1886[2], Senj 1908[3]) should also be noted especially for the part they played in the development of literary Croatian in Dalmatia. Parčić knew the vernacular spoken in Čakavic Dalmatia very well and recorded many words pertaining to local speeches in his dictionaries, enlarged in their subsequent editions, which thus serve as a source for the study of Croatian dialects and etymology. To judge by the frequency ot their editions, Parčić's dictionaries gained greater circulation than any other book of their kind.

The work on the first major monolingual all-Croatian dictionary started in 1866, when the Serbian philologist Đuro Daničić (1825-82) came to Zagreb as Secretary of the newly-founded South Slav Academy of Fine Arts and Science. He immediately began work on the Dictionary of the Croatian or Serbian Language (*Rječnik hrvatskog ili srpskog jezika*), edited by the Zagreb Academy between 1866 and 1976. The Dictionary's first volume had been published in 1881, its last in 1976. The purpose of Daničić's cooperation with his Zagreb colleagues in the Academy was to avoid new and unnecessary differences between Croatian and Serbian and, if possible, to try to close the gaps between the two languages. Daničić was the most fervent partisan and supporter of Vuk Karadižić's views on language reform, which he set forth in the survey of the Dictionary (of the Academy) (*Ogled Rječnika*) in 1878.

The first volume, published in 1881, and subsequent volumes of this dictionary were elaborated strictly in accordance with Karadžić's programme, which was often contrary to the Croat literary tradition. Thus the lexical stock of the rich Kajkavic literature, which had flourished in Northern Croatia since the 16th century, has been largely omitted from this 23 quarto volume Dictionary, while its first volumes make scarcely any reference to modern Croat literature. In this historical, but not pandialectal, comprehensive dictionary, the emphasis is laid more upon the origin and history of words than on their current usage. Such a diachronic overall strategy of the Dictionary of the Academy based on historical principles is alien to the purpose of synchronic description. However, it is the most compendious and scholarly dictionary of the Croatian language with the scientific goal of completeness and rigour in its chosen area. It has twenty-three quarto volumes (each volume has 960 pages) and contains about 300,000 lexical items. To amend deficiencies and correct errors, many Croatian words, omitted in previously published volumes, have been recorded in its Supplements and the hitherto neglected sources for its compilation were more thorougly exploited.

A well-known philologist, Tomislav Maretić (1854-1938), the fourth consecutive editor of the Dictionary of the Academy of Zagreb, was highly critical of Daničić's omission of Kajkavic terms from the Dictionary. To make up for this deficiency, the Historico-Philological Department of the Zagreb Academy decided in 1936 to edit a separate Dictionary of Kajkavic dialect. However, the actual work on the compilation of this dictionary only started in 1973. The dictionary will consist of two quarto volumes and will contain all the terms of literary Kajkavic, from the 16th century to the present day. Unfortunately, the words of the contemporary Kajkavic vernacular will not be included in this dictionary.

By the turn of the century another monolingual Croatian dictionary (*Rječnik hrvatskog jezika*, Zagreb, 1901, 2 vols. VII, 951, 884 pp.) was compiled by Ivan Broz, who died in 1893, and his uncle, Franjo Iveković. In this dictionary, eighty per cent of the (52,279) entries have been taken from Štokavic folk poetry, popular tales, proverbs and other gnomic expressions, while many Čakavic and Kajkavic terms used in contemporary Standard Croatian have been left out. Moreover, thousands of words of 19th century literary Croatian have not been entered in this dictionary. In neglecting the synchronic study of *kaj* and *ča* dialects and of contemporary literary language the authors held, as did Herman Paul (1846-1921) in his *Principles of History of Language*, that only a historical study of language had scholarly and scientific value. However, Broz-Iveković's Dictionary is abundant in synonyms and phraseology and every lexical item has a prosodic mark written above it. It has played a great part in the formation of literary Koine and is still consulted and used.

In 1922 Vladimir Mažuranić completed his *Prinosi za hrvatski pravno-povjestni rječnik* (Contributions to Croatian Legal and Historical Dictionary) (2 vols., XIX+1751, Zagreb, 1908-1922). This work contains all the terms that appear in legal documents written in Croatia between the thirteenth and the nineteenth centuries. It gives an analytical summary of the entire political and legal history of Croatia as recorded in

27

charters, laws, statutes, contracts, wills, and courts injunctions written in Croatian.

Among monolingual all-Croatian dictionaries one should also mention Iso Velikanović's *Šta je šta* (Zagreb, 1938, X+685 pp.), a pictorial Croatian dictionary which may be compared with the German *Bildwörterbuch Duden*. It also contains a vast technological nomenclature. In 1934 Marcel Kušar brought out his monolingual phraseological dictionary *Narodno Blago* (People's Folk Treasure), a collection of locutions and expressions systematically classified under different headings.

Divković's monolingual *Dictionary of the Croatian Language* completed in 1923, remained in manuscript and has never been published.

Another monolingual dictionary is *Rječnik hrvatskosrpskog književnog jezika* (Zagreb 1967, Vol. I A-F 747 pp.; Vol. II G-K 840 pp.). Only two volumes covering the letters A-K of a projected six volumes have so far been published. The publication has been interrupted due to 'Serbo-Croatian controversies'.

Barring unforeseen events, the most comprehensive dictionary to date of Literary Croatian (*Rječnik hrvatskog književnog jezika*) will be published in the near future by the Yugoslav Academy in Zagreb. The work on this dictionary was started in 1948 by Julije Benešić. After his death in 1957 the work on it was interrupted for political reasons under the pressure of public authorities and was resumed a few years ago by Josip Hamm.

By the same token, under the pressure of political authorities, the publication of *Orthography of the Croatian Literary Language*, a spelling dictionary of 80,000 lexical items, compiled by Vladimir Anić and Josip Silić, which was due to appear in 1981 has been delayed (Pavičić, 1982:6).

The 19th and 20th centuries interlingual dictionaries, that were brought out in Croatia, had a far greater stock of contemporary Croatian words than were to be found in the all-Croatian dictionaries, but the compilers of the Croatian dictionaries, strangely enough, never took full advantage of these sources. Let us note that Benešić's Croatian-Polish

Dictionary (*Hrvatsko-Poljski Rječnik*, Zagreb 1949, 1304 pp.) has 66,170 Croatian entries, that is to say 10,891 lexical items more than Broz-Iveković's Dictionary of 1901.

Although the *Dictionary of the Yugoslav Academy* and Mažuranić's *Contributions to Croatian Legal and Historical Dictionary* are partly etymological dictionaries, the first over-all etymological dictionary, namely Petar Skok's *Etimologijski rječnik hrvatskog ili srpskog jezika* (Zagreb, Yugoslav Academy, 4 vols.), came out only in 1971-74. Skok started working on it in 1942 and when he died in 1956 the manuscript of the dictionary was left in longhand. In 1961 Valentin Putanec resumed the work on the dictionary and, after a thorough revision, prepared it for printing. Though it is the largest etymological dictionary in the Slavic world, it is also less Slavic than its counterparts in other Slavic languages, since it contains more etymons of Turkish, Albanian, Modern Greek (Katharevusa and Demotic), Italian and Old Dalmatian than of Slavic origin. Generally speaking, this dictionary bears the imprint of its author, who was first and foremost ' a scholar of Romance languages and Balkan Latinism and only afterwards a Slavicist.

The 20th century Croatian lexicography is abounding in general-purpose and specialized bilingual dictionaries: German, English, Italian, French and Russian especially.

In conclusion, it is worth mentioning the achievements of *Leksikografski Zavod* (The Institute for Lexicography) in Zagreb founded in 1950. Under the management of Miroslav Krleža (1893-1981) it published a series of reference books: fifteen different general-knowledge and specialized encyclo-paedias, each of several volumes, and twenty-four general-purpose and special subject lexicons in one volume.

NOTES

1 Croatian has three main dialects named after the different forms of the interrogative pronoun 'what', which is *što* in *što* dialect, *kaj* in *kaj* dialect, and *ča* in *ča* dialect. The Čakavic (or *ča* dialect) is spoken in Southern Croatia, on the Dalmatian coast, and on the islands.

The Kajkavic is spoken in Northern Croatia, in the regions around Zagreb. Štokavic, the most extensive dialect is spoken in Bosnia, Herzegovina, Dalmatia, Slavonia, Bačka, Kordun, Banija and Lika. It is this *što* dialect that has become the basis of standard literary Croatian, but *kaj* and *ča* dialects have played a part in the formation of the Croat koine based on *što* dialect.

2 Illyria was an ancient country situated along the East coast of the Adriatic, and Illyrian, an extinct Indo-European language, once spoken in the Balkans, was probably allied with Albanian. Since the Croats settled in the Roman province of Illyricum, during the 7th century A.D., the term 'lingua illyrica' was often used to designate the Croatian language and 'Illyricus' a native of Croatia.

For a brief historical survey of the name of the Croatian language through the centuries from its origins up to the 20th century see:

a) Ostojić, Ivan, *Kako su Hrvati nazivali svoj jezik*, in *Kolo* 1-2 (Zagreb) 1971, 93-118.

b) Zelić-Bučan, Benedikta, *Nekoliko izvornih svjedočanstava o hrvatskom nazivu hrvatskog jezika*, in *Kolo* No 4 (Zagreb) 1970, 480-484.

c) Zelić-Bučan, Benedikta, *Narodni naziv hrvatskog jezika tijekom hrvatske povijesti*, in *Jezik* XIX (Zagreb) 1971-72, 1-18, 38-48.

3 Florence's Academy of the Chaff (*Academia della Crusca*) was founded in 1583 by a handful of local *literati*, perhaps *bons vivants* would be more apt. The academy eventually decided its mission was to settle the argument as to how   Italian should develop (*questione della lingua*) and to stop the erosion of the Florentine language by compiling Europe's first modern dictionary. The first volume of *Vocabolario* came out in 1612 and took note of many of Pietro Bembo's recommendations, who maintained that classical Tuscan models should be followed, Petrarch in poetry and Boccaccio in prose. It was later to be used as a model for German, Catalan and French (whose Académie was founded for the same reason in 1635). It was the Florentine dictionary which first used "occurrences" as they call them, that is citations from acceptable authors. However, the compilers of *Vocabolario* decided from the beginning (four complete editions of the dictionary have been published) that they would be very cautious about

accepting any word which had not been used by Dante (1265-1321), Petrarch (1304-1374), or Boccaccio (1313-75). The mere existence of the Florentine dictionary probably contributed enormously to Florentine becoming, during the Renaissance, not only the language of educated Italians but the second language of educated Europeans.

REFERENCES

Baudoin de Courtenay, J. I., 1888. *Das Slavische in den Werken von B. Georgievics*, in *Archiv für Slavische Philologie*.

Brlek, M.I., 1980. *Joakim Stulli (1730-1817)*. *Anali Zavoda za povijesne znanosti IC JAZU* u Dubrovniku, Vol. XVIII, Dubrovnik 1980, 221-249.

Brozek, J., 1973. *Pchychologia of Marcus Marulus (1450-1524), Evidence in printed works and estimated date of origin*. Episteme (Milano) 7, 125-131.

Cartelazzo, M. 1980. *I dialetti e la dialettologia in Italia (fino al 1800)*. Tübingen, Gunter Narr Verlag (Series Ars Linguistica 4).

De Toni, E. 1925. *Il Libro dei Semplici*, Roma, Scuola Tipografica Pio X.

Dukat., V., 1905. *Jambrešićev Lexicon latinum*, in *Rad Jugosl. Akademije*, Vol. 162.

Galić, P., 1981. *Un manuale di conversazione italo-croato (Venezia 1804)*, in *Studi di Grammatica Italiana*, Vol. 10, 51-61.

Hamm, J., 1952. *Glose u Radonovoj bibliji*, in *Slovo* 1, 19-33.

Jonke, Lj., 1949. *"Dikcionar" Adama ;Patačića*, in *Rad JAZU*, Vol. 275, 71-115.

Kidrič, F., 1920. *Bartholomaeus Gjorgjević, biographische und bibliographische Zusammenfassung.*

Kosor, J., 1975. *Mali konverzacioni rječnik "Zvanik novi"*, in *Čakavska rič* 5, No. 2, 55-65.

Lapointe, F.H., 1972. *Who originated the term 'psychology?'*, in *Journal of the History of Behavioral Sciences* 8, 328-335.

Luetić, J., 1965. *Naša pomorska terminologija u A. Jalovom "Glossaire nautique" iz 1848 g.*, in *Ljetopis Jugosl. Akademije*, Zagreb, Vol. 61, 248-254.

Melich, J., 1906. *A magyar szotarirodalom*, in *Nyelvtudomanyi Közlemenyek* 36.

Minio, M., 1953. *Il quattrocentesco codice 'Rinio' integralmente rivendicato al medico Roccabonella*, in *Atti dell'Istituto Veneto di Scienze, lettere ed arti.*

Nametak, A., 1968. *Rukopisni tursko-hrvatskosrpski rječnici*, in *Građa za povijest književnosti hrvatske*, Vol. 29, 231-380.

Nametak, A., 1978. *Tri rukopisa "Makbuli Arifa" ("Potur Šahidija ")*, in *Anali Gazi Husrev-begove biblioteke* 5-6, 145-164.

Pajk, M., 1889. in *Archiv für Slavische Philologie*, Berlin, XXI, 639-40.

Pavičić, J., 1982. *Pravopis nije za vječnost*, in Zagreb daily *Vjesnik* (2 March).

Petr, J., 1973. *Italsko-čakavská jazyková příručka 2 r. 1527*, in *Slavia* (Prague) 44-67.

Pohl, H.D., 1976. *Das Italienisch-Kroatische Glossar, MS Selden Supra 95, Die Österreichische Akademie der Wissenschaften*, Wien.

Putanec, V., 1971. *Apostile uz Dictionarium Quinque Nobilissimarum Europae Linguarum Fausta Vrančića*, in *Čakavska rič*, 2, 5-18.

Putanec, V., 1979[a]. *Talijansko-Hrvatski i Hrvatsko-Talijanski Rječnik Petra Lupisa Valentiana (Ankona 1527)*, in *Filologija* (Zagreb), No. 9, 101-138.

Putanec, V., 1979[b]. *Mali diferencijalni hrvatsko-slovenski rječnici iz 1578, 1584 i 1592*, in *Rad JAZU*, Vol. 376, 159-215.

Putanec, V., 1979[c]. *'Zvanik Talijansko-Hrvatski' (1655, 1703, 1737, 1804)*, in *Rasprave zavoda za jezik*, JAZU, Vol. 4-5, 41-60.

Rešetar, M., 1904, in *Archiv für Slavische Philologie*, Berlin XXVI, 358-366.

Schmaus, A., 1956. *Sigismundus Gelenius und sein Lexicon symphonum (1537)*, in *Festsch. für Max Vasmer zum 70. Geburtstag*, 434-444.

Vončina, J., 1973. *Leksikografski rad Ivana Belostenca*, in the reprint edition of *Gazophylacium*, Zagreb, Liber, Vol. 2, III-XLIII.

Vončina, J., 1979. *Vrančićev rječnik*, in *Filologija* (Zagreb) 9, 139-144.

OPERA NVOVA CHE
INSEGNA A PARLARE LA LINGVA
SCHIAVONESCHA ALLI GRANDI
ALLI PICOLI ET ALLE
DONNE.

ET SIMILMENTE LA DITTA OPERA
Insegna alli Schiauoni A parlare bono et corretto
Italiano.

ANCORA LA DITTA OPERA INSEGNA
A legere a chi non sa,et a quelli che sano vno poco legere
Lo ditto ammaistramento li sara di molta
vtilita,per caxon delle parole
et silabe scrite in
Schiauonescho

Con Gratia et Priuilegio.

M. D. XXVII.

The titlepage of Lupis Valentiano's *Opera nuova* . . . (Ancona 1527)

LEXICVM

SYMPHONVM

QVO QVATVOR LINGVARVM EV/
ropæ familiarium, Græcæ scilicet, Latinæ, Germa/
nicæ ac Sclauinicæ concordia consonantiaǵ
indicatur, per Sigismundum Gelenium
quantum per ocium licuit non
oscitanter editum.

FRO   BEN.

BASILEAE ANNO M D XXXVII

The titlepage of Gelenius's *Lexicum symphonum . . .* (Basle 1537)

MONOLINGUAL DICTIONARIES

GENERAL ENCYCLOPEDIC DICTIONARIES
and
LEXICONS

Enciklopedija Hrvatske Povijesti i Kulture. Zagreb, Školska
knjiga, 1980, 1 vol. VIII + 912 pp. Chief ed.: Igor Karaman
Encyclopedic Dictionary of Croatian History and Civil-
ization. 1

Enciklopedija Jugoslavije. Zagreb, 1955-71, 8 vols. 5400 pp.
Chief ed.: Miroslav Krleža
Contains over 18,000 articles with major emphasis on
Yugoslavia. 2

Enciklopedija Leksikografskog zavoda — opća. First ed.:
Zagreb, 1955-64; 7 vols., Chief ed.: Marko Kostrenčić, Miroslav
Krleža (vols. 1-2); Marko Kostrenčić, Miljenko Protega (vols.
3-7). 2nd ed.: 1966-9, 6 vols., 4364 pp.; 3rd ed.: 1975-81, 8 vols.
A popular version of *Enciklopedija Jugoslavije.* A general
encyclopedia in the Croatian language; valuable for its
many biographies of Croatians not elsewhere available.
It is also strong in biography of 20th century personalities
and celebrities. 3

Filipović, Marijan. *Đački Leksikon.* Čakovec, Zrinski, 1978.
Contains 10,000 entries, 442 drawings.
School Lexicon. 4

Getz-Gets, Franjo. *Leksikon hrvatski.* Zlatar, 1903, 70 pp. 5

Hrvatska enciklopedija. Zagreb, Konzorcija Hrvatske enciklopedije, 1941-45. 5 vols. Editor: Mate Ujević.
Ceased publication with vol. 5 which covered the subjects
from *Dil* to *Elektrika.* A general Croatian encyclopedia
extremely valuable for its biographies of famous Croatians
despite its incomplete status. 6

Leksikon jugoslavenskog leksikografskog zavoda. Zagreb, 1974, 1 vol. 1095 pp. Ed.: Nada Bogdanov et al.
Contains 45,000 items; 6,000 illustrations. 7

Leksikon Minerva. Zagreb, 1936, 1584 columns. Editor: Gustav Šamšalović.
A general Croatian encyclopedia that includes an important number of Slavic biographical sketches. 8

Stanojević, Stanoje. *Narodna enciklopedija srpsko-hrvatsko-slovenačka.* Zagreb, Bibliografski zavod, 1925-29. 4 vols.
The first encyclopedia published in Yugoslavia. It had two editions, one in the Latin alphabet and the other in the Cyrillic. 9

Sveznadar—Nauka i znanje u riječi i slici. Zagreb, Seljačka sloga, 1954, 878 pp. Chief ed.: Nada Sremec. 2nd ed. under the title *Priručni leksikon.* Zagreb, Znanje, 1959, 1103 pp. 3rd ed. 1967, 1021 pp. Ed.: Milan Selaković & Ivo Vrančić. 10

Svijet oko nas. Enciklopedija za djecu i omladinu. Vol. 1 (A-M), Zagreb, ŠK, 1960, 264 pp. Vol. 2 (N-Ž) Zagreb, ŠK, 1962, 266 pp. 9th ed.: Vol. 1 (A-M), 1984. Chief ed.: Juraj Bukša.
Encyclopedia for youth and children. 11

Tarczay-Korlević. *Jugoslovenski leksikon.* Zagreb, 1931. 12

Zoch, Ivan; Josip Mencin. *Hrvatska Enciklopedija — Priručni rječnik sveobćeg znanja.* Vol. 1 (A-Bžedusi), Osijek, 1887, 619 pp. Vol. 2 (C-Gzel), Osijek, 1890, 576 pp.
Croatian encyclopedia of general knowledge. 13

DIALECT

Boryś, Wiestaw. *Budowa rzeczowników w tekstach czakawakich xv i xvi w.* Wrocław, 1969, 290 pp. 14

Hraste, Mate; Petar Šimunović; Reinhold Olesch. *Čakavisch-deutsches Lexicon.* Köln - Wien: Böhlau, 1979, LX+, 1416 Sp. (Slavistische Forschungen. 25, I)
    Dictionary of Čakavic dialect of the islands of Brač, Hvar and Vis. 15

Jurišić, Blaž. *Rječnik govora otoka Vrgade.* Dio I: Zagreb, JAZU, 1966, 126 pp. Dio II: Rječnik, 1973, 255 pp. 16

Rječnik hrvatskoga kajkavskoga književnog jezika. Zagreb, JAZU, 1984. Vol. I A-C(cenina), 65-240 pp.
    Contains ca. 3400 entries. 17

Turina, Zvonimir; Anton Šepić. *Rječnik čakavskih izraza s područja Bakarca i Škrljeva.* Rijeka, Riječko književno i naučno društvo, 1978, 231 pp. 18

ETYMOLOGY

Katančić, M. Petar. *Pravoslovnik. Etymologicon illyricum, ad leges philologiae dialecto bosnensi exactum.* Covering the letters A-S (*Svemoguć*). Compiled around 1815-24. 1473 pages in manuscript containing 53,000 entries.
    Croatian etymological dictionary. 19

Skok, Petar. *Etimologijski rječnik hrvatskoga ili srpskoga jezika.* Zagreb, JAZU, 1971-74, 4 vols. Vol. 1 (A-J) XXXVIII + 788 pp. Vol. 2 (K-Poni) 7oo pp. Vol. 3 (Poni-Ž) 703 pp. Vol. 4 (Index) 837 pp.
    Etymological dictionary of Croatian or Serbian. 20

Šetka, Jeronim. *Hrvatska kršćanska terminologija.* Makarska, Franjevačka visoka bogoslovija, 1940-1965. Dio I, *Hrvatski kršćanski termini grčkoga podrijetla.* 1940, X + 206 pp. Dio II, *Hrvatski kršćanski termini latinskoga podrijetla.* 1964, 233 pp. Dio III, *Hrvatski kršćanski termini slavenskog podrijetla.*

1965, 286 pp. 2nd ed. *Hrvatska kršćanska terminologija*, Split, Marija, 1976, 366 pp.
Croatian Christian terminology of Greek, Latin and Slavonic origin. 21

FOREIGN WORDS

Filipović, Marijan. *Džepni rječnik stranih riječi*. Zagreb, Borba, 1962, 319 pp. 2nd ed: Varaždin, Novinsko i Štamparsko Poduzeće, 1965, 422 pp. 22

Id. *Mali rječnih stranih riječi*. Zagreb, Borba, 1960, 154 pp. 23

Id. *Rječnik stranih riječi*. Zagreb, Mladost, 1983, 400 pp. 24

Klaić, Bratoljub. *Rječnik stranih riječi, izraza i kratica*. Zagreb, Zora 1951, vii + 714 pp; 2nd ed. 1958, 1,371 pp; 3rd ed. 1962, xv + 1608 pp; 4 ed. 1966, xvi + 1348 pp; 5 ed. 1974, 1,440 pp; 6 ed. Zagreb, Nakladni Zavod Hrvatske, 1978, viii + 1,456 pp. 25

Klaić, Željko. *Rječnik stranih riječi*. Zagreb, Matica hrvatska, 1970, viii + 320 pp. 26

Kovčić, Dragutin (Prica, Ognjen). *Rječnik stranih riječi*. Zagreb, 1938, 214 pp. 2 ed. 1940, 253 pp., 3 ed. 1945. 27

Kurelac, Fran. *Vlaške riječi u jeziku našem*. Rad JAZU (20) 1872 28

Maretić, Tomo. *Ruske i češke riječi u književnom hrvatskom jeziku*. Rad JAZU, (108) 1892. 29

Prica, Ognjen. *Rječnik stranih riječi, izraza i kratica*. 3 rev. enl. ed. Zagreb, Nakladni Zavod Hrvatske, 1945, 243 pp. 30

Šeringer, Vinko. *Priručni rječnik tuđih riječi i fraza.* Zagreb, L. Hartman (St. Kugli), 1889, XII+169 pp.; 2 ed. 1906 XV+241; 3 ed. 1916; 4 ed. 1920; 5 ed. 1928, 292 pp.; 6 ed. 1934; 7 ed. 1942. 31

Id. *Rječnik stranih riječi.* Zagreb, Zadružna štampa, 1965, 405 pp. 32

Zore, Luka. *Dubrovačke tuđinke.* Beograd, Spomenik SAN, 1885, vol. XXVI. 33

HISTORICAL

Daničić, Djuro. *Korijeni s riječima od njih postalijem u hrvatskom ili srpskom jeziku.* Zagreb, Hartman, 1877, iv + 369 pp. 34

Dictionnaire Illyrien. Klagenfurt, 1744. 35

Kuzmanović, Mladen. *Rječnik i komentar Balada Petrice Kerempuha Miroslava Krleže.* Zagreb, Liber, 1972, 193 pp.
Glossary to M. Krleža's *Ballads of Petrica Kerempuh.* 36

Mažuranić, Ivan; Antun Mažuranić. Osmana Gundulićeva rječnik. Zagreb, 1844.
Glossary to Gundulić's *Osman.* 37

Mažuranić, Vladimir. *Prinosi za hrvatski pravno-povjestni rječnik.* Zagreb, JAZU, 1908-1923, XIX+1751 pp.. Reprint, Zagreb, Informator, 1975.
It is also partly an etymological dictionary. 38

Stachowski, Stanislaw. *Wyrazy serbo-chorwackie w 'Thesaurus Polyglottus' H. Megisera, 1603.* Wrocław, Ossolineum, 1969, 167 pp. 39

KINSHIP

Barišić, Mate. *Rodbinski nazivi.* Split, 1937, 14 pp.
Croatian kinship terminology. 40

Ivanišević, Jožo, F. *Narodni nazivi rodbine i srodbine.* 2 ed:
Sarajevo, 1931. 41

Tanocki, Franjo. *Rječnik rodbinskih naziva.* Osijek, 1983,
143 pp.
Dictionary of Croatian kinship terminology. 42

Zovko, Ivan. *Rodbinski nazivi u Herceg-Bosni.* In: Zbornik
za narodni život i običaje južnih Slavena, Knj. VII. Zagreb,
JAZU, 1902. 43

LANGUAGE

Benešić, Julije. *Rječnik hrvatskog književnog jezika.*
Preserved in manuscript, from *A* to *Serenada*; from
Serenada to *Z* compiled by Josip Hamm. To be published
by Jugoslav Academy in Zagreb.
Dictionary of Literary Croatian. 44

Čubelić, Tvrtko. *Usmene narodne poslovice, pitalice, zago-
netke.* Zagreb, 1975.
Collection of gnomic expressions. 45

Daničić, Djuro; Matija Valjavec; Pero Budmani; Tomislav
Maretić; Stjepan Musulin; Slavko Pavešić et al. *Rječnik hrvatskog ili srpskog jezika.* Zagreb, 1880-1976, 23 vols., each
volume has 960 pp.
The most compendious dictionary of the Croatian
language, ca. 300,000 words. 46

Divković, Mirko. *Rječnik hrvatskog jezika.*
Preserved in manuscript, completed in 1923. Dictionary
of the Croatian language. 47

Iveković, Franjo; Ivan Broz. *Rječnik hrvatskoga jezika.* Zagreb,
Štamparija Karla Albrechta, 1901, 2 vols. Vol. 1 (A-O) VII +
951 pp. Vol. 2 (P-Ž) 884 pp.
Dictionary of the Croatian language. 48

Kumičić, Eugenij. *Frazarij. Zbirka narodnih uzrečica, poslovica
i pjesničkih riječi.* 292 pp + 21.
Manuscript kept in Zagreb University Library (R 5543).
Collection of gnomic expressions. 49

Kušar, Marcel. *Narodno blago.* Split - Ljubljana, 1934. 2nd ed.
Zagreb, Društvo književnih prevodilaca Hrvatske, 219 pp.
A phraseological dictionary. 50

Matešić, Josip et al. *Frazeološki rječnik hrvatskoga ili srpskog
jezika.* Zagreb, Školska knjiga, 1982, xx + 808 pp.
More than 30,000 entries.
Croatian phraseological dictionary. 51

Rječnik hrvatskosrpskog književnog jezika. Vols. 1-2, Zagreb,
Matica hrvatska; Novi Sad, Matica srpska, 1967. Vol. 1 (A-F)
747 pp. Vol. 2 (G-K), 840 pp.
Only vols. 1-2 covering the letters A-K of a projected
6 vols. have so far been published. 52

Velikanović, Iso; Nikola Andrić. *Šta je šta; Stvarni hrvatski
rječnik u slikama.* Zagreb, Minerva, 1938, x + 685 pp.
Croatian pictorial *Duden.* Contains a vast technological
nomenclature. 53

ONOMASTICS

Administrativno-teritorijalna podjela i imenik naseljenih mjesta Narodne Republike Hrvatske. Zagreb, Statistički ured Narodne Republike Hrvatske, 1957, 346 pp.

Grujić, M. Radoslav. *Plemenski rječnik ličko-krbavske županije,* In Zbornik za narodni život i običaje Južnih Slavena, V. 21, 1917, pp. 273-364.

Karaś, Mieczysław. *Toponimia Wysp Elafickich na Adriatyku.* Wrocław, Zakład Zarodowy im. Ossolinskich, 1968, 142 pp.

Putanec, Valentin; Petar Šimunović et al. *Leksik Prezimena Socijalističke Republike Hrvatske.* Zagreb, Institut za jezik JAZU - Matica hrvatska, 1976, in-folio, xiv + 772 pp.

Sabljar, Vinko. *Miestopisni riečnik kraljevinah Dalmacije, Hervatske i Slavonije.* Zagreb, 1886, 540 pp.

Smodlaka, Josip. *Imena mesta i meštana na tlu Jugoslavije.* Split, Novo Doba, 1946, vii + 160 pp.

Šarčević, Ambrozio. *Tolmač izvornih književnih i zemljopisnih jugoslavenskih riči.* Subotica, 1870, v + 186 pp.

Šimundić, Mate. *Rječnik osobnih imena hrvatskog ili srpskog jezika.* Split, Logos, 1984, 1000 pp.

Šimunović, Petar. *Toponimija otoka Brača.* Supetar, Skupština općine Brač — Savjet za prosvjetu i kulturu, 1972, xx + 318, 21 pp.

ORTHOGRAPHIC DICTIONARIES
AND LANGUAGE USAGE COUNSELLORS

Andrić, Nikola. *Branič jezika hrvatskoga.* Zagreb, 1911, 148 pp. 63

Babić, Stjepan; Božidar Finka; Milan Moguš. *Hrvatski Pravopis.* Zagreb - London, 1972, xvi + 343. 64

Balenović, Vid. *Rječnik riječi sa suglasnicima č i ć.* Zagreb, Seljačka Sloga, 1954, 93 pp. 65

Boranić, Dragutin. *Pravopis hrvatskoga ili srpskoga jezika.* Zagreb, 1921, 242 pp. 3 ed: Zagreb, 1936, 190 pp. 9 rev. ed: Zagreb, 1947, 207 pp. 10 ed: Zagreb, Školska Knjiga, 1951, 213 pp. 66

Brabec, Ivan. *Sto jezičnih savjeta.* Zagreb, Školske Novine, 1982, 181 pp. 2nd ed: 1984, 181 pp. 67

Broz, Ivan. *Hrvatski pravopis.* Zagreb, Nakl. Kr. hrv.-slav.-dalm. zemaljske vlade, 1892, vii + 130 pp. 2nd ed. 1893, xii + 133 pp. 3rd ed. 1904, 214 pp. 4th ed. 1906, 214 pp. 5th ed. 1911, 228 pp. 6th ed. 1915, 239 pp. 68

Cerovac, Mirko. *Jezični savjetnik za uredske kadrove.* Zagreb, Birotehnika, 1958, 250 pp. 2 ed. 1960, 226 pp. 69

Id. *Poslovni jezik.* Zagreb, Informator, 1964, 229 pp. 70

Cipra, Franjo; Bratoljub Klaić et al. *Hrvatski pravopis.* Zagreb, Naklada odjela Hrvatske državne tiskare, 1944, 459 pp. 71

Ćeklić, Vaso. *Vještina pisanja.* Zagreb, 1962, 137 pp. 72

Esih, Ivan. *Hrvatski pravopisni rječnik.* Zagreb, Naklada "Tipografije", 1940, 54 pp. (in two columns).
Contains also kinship terminology. 73

Gaj, Ljudevit. *Kratka osnova horvatsko-slavenskog pravopisaňa.* Budim, 1830, 27 pp. Reprint, Zagreb, Međunarodni slavistički centar SR Hrvatske, 1983. 74

Gavazzi, Milovan. *Pravopisni rječnik s pravopisnim pravilima.* Zagreb, St. Kugli, 1921, 138 pp. 75

Giamagnich, Raymond. *Nauk za pisati dobro latinskiema slovima rieci yesika slovinskoga.* Venezia. M. Ginammi, 1639, 60 pp. 76

Jambrešić, Andrija. *Manuductio ad croaticam orthographiam.* Zagreb, 1732. 77

Id. *Kratki navuk za pravopisanje horvatsko za potrebnost narodnih škol.* Zagreb, 1779. 78

Jonke, Ljudevit; Mihailo Stevanović. *Pravopis hrvatskosrpskog jezika.* Zagreb, Matica hrvatska, 6 ed., 1968, 274 pp. 79

Klaić, Bratoljub. *Koriensko pisanje.* Zagreb, HIBZ, 1942, 136 pp. 80

Kosor, Karlo. *Bilješke o jeziku suvremenih hrvatskih pisaca.* Split, 2nd ed., 1979, 112 pp. 81

Mahanović, Marko. *Obşervationes circa Croaticam orthographiam.* 1814. 82

Maretić, Tomislav. *Hrvatski ili srpski jezični savjetnik za sve one, koji žele dobro govoriti i pisati književnim našim jezikom.* Zagreb, Hartman, 1924, xxxi + 205 pp. 83

Pavešić, Slavko et. al. *Jezični savjetnik s gramatikom.* Zagreb, Institut za jezik JAZU — Matica hrvatska, 1971, 446 (5) pp. 84

Pravopis hrvatskosrpskoga književnog jezika. Zagreb, Matica hrvatska — Novi Sad, Matica srpska, 1960, 882 pp.
    Latin and Cyrillic editions. 85

Rožić, Vatroslav. *Barbarizmi u hrvatskom jeziku.* Zemun, 1904, 2 ed. Zagreb 1908. 3 ed. 1913. 86

Soljačić, Marko. *Jezični i stilistički savjetnik.* **Zagreb, Naklada školskih knjiga i tiskanica Savske banovine,** 1939, 182 pp. 87

Ujčić, Vitomir. *Hrvatskosrpski književni jezik i pravopis.* Pula, 1955, 44 pp. 88

Vidović, Radovan. *O suvremenom stanju našega jezika masovne komunikacije. Mali rječnik naše suvremene nepismenosti.* Split, Biblioteka Školskog vjesnika, No 3, 1968, 71 pp. 89

Id. *Kako ne valja, kako valja pisati.* Zagreb, 2nd enlarged edition, 1969, 243 pp. 90

Id. *Jezični savjeti.* Split, Logos, 1983, 89 pp. 91

Zore, Luka. *Paljetkovanje.* Rad JAZU, knj. 108, 110, 114, 115, 138, 170. 92

REVERSE

Matešić, Josip. *Rückläufiges Wörterbuch des Serbokroatischen.* Wiesbaden, Otto Harrassowitz, 1965-67; xi+228, 244, 240, vii+250 pp. 93

SLANG

Sabljak, Tomislav. *Rječnik šatrovačkog govora.* Zagreb, Globus, 1982, 214 pp. 94

Šahinović-Ekremov, Munir. *Riječnik jugoslavenskih šatrovaca.* Zagreb, Tisak štamparije Gaj, s.a., 26 pp. 94a

SPECIAL AND SUBJECT
DICTIONARIES

AGRICULTURE, AGRONOMY, FORESTRY, HUNTING

Bolić, P. *Slovar vinodělca*. Budim, 1818.
Dictionary of viticulture. 95

Ettinger, Josip. *Šumarsko-lovački leksikon*. Zagreb, Nakl.
Kr. sveučilišne knjižare Franje Suppana, 1898, 438 pp.
Lexicon of forestry and hunting. 96

Kišpatić, Dragutin; Viktor D. Sonnefeld. *Rječnik hrvatsko-srpskoga govora lovačkoga*. Osijek, 1926, 162 pp.
Dictionary of the language of hunting. 97

Poljoprivredna enciklopedija. Zagreb, Leksikografski zavod,
1967-73, 3 vols., 2100 pp. Chief ed.: Mladen Josifović.
Encyclopedia of agriculture and agronomy. 98

Šumarska enciklopedija. Zagreb, Leksikografski zavod, 1959-
63, 2 vols., 1568 pp. Chief ed.: Aleksandar Ugrenović;
Zvonimir Potočić (vol. 1), Zvonimir Potočić (vol. 2). 2 ed. 1980.
Encyclopedia of forestry. 99

Šumarski priručnik. Zagreb, Poljoprivredni nakladni zavod,
1946, 2 vols., 1582+xv+xxx pp. Ed.: Josip Šafar.
Manual of forestry. 100

COMMERCE and ECONOMY

Dabčević-Kučar, Savka et al. *Mali ekonomski rječnik*. Zagreb,
Nakladno poduzeće Glasa rada, 1953, xv+404 pp.
Dictionary of economy. 101

Deželić, Stanko. *Terminologija trgovačkih znanosti*. Zagreb,
1922, 280+xvi pp.
Terminology of commerce. 102

Id. *Trgovački leksikon*. Zagreb, Naklada "Bibliografskog zavoda", 1925, viii+433 pp. (in two columns).
Lexicon of commerce. 103

Dragičević, Adolf. *Leksikon političke ekonomije*. Zagreb, Informator, 1965, 2 vols., 388, 122 pp. 104

Dutković, Ivo. *Stenografski rječnik za trgovačku praksu, zbirka pokrata*. Zagreb, Naklada Knjižare St. Kugli, 1926, 256 pp.
Dictionary of commercial shorthand. 105

Herkov, Zlatko. *Građa za financijsko-pravni rječnik feudalne epohe Hrvatske*. Zagreb, JAZU, 1956. Vol. I, vii+535 pp. Vol. II, 620 pp. 106

Jelčić, Božidar. *Rječnik javnih financija i financijskog prava*. Zagreb, Informator, 1981, 368 pp. 107

Kohn, Feliks. *Trgovački i pravni leksikon*. Osijek, 1937, 1085 pp. (in two columns).
Lexicon of commerce and law. 108

Leksikon vanjske trgovine. Zagreb, Informator, 1965. 109

Nomenklatura robe. Zagreb, 1964. 110

Privredni leksikon. Zagreb, Informator, 1961, 787 pp. Ed.: Martin Dobrinčić et al. 111
Lexicon of economy.

Šarinić, Josip. *Pravno-ekonomski leksikon*. Zagreb, ŠK, 1977, iv+304 pp.
Lexicon of legal and economic terminology. 112

Urbani, Milutin. *Leksikon trgovačke i gospodarske robe*. Zagreb, Prosvjetna nakladna zadruga, 1925, 266 pp. (in two columns).
Lexicon of merchandise. 113

47

Zadružni leksikon FNRJ. I-II, Zagreb, Zadružna štampa, 1956-57, 1552 pp.   114

FINE ARTS
Music

Chudoba, Dinko. *Muzički rječnik*. Zagreb, IBI, 1958, 216 pp.
Dictionary of music.   115

Muzička enciklopedija. Zagreb, 1957-74. Chief ed.: Josip Andreis, 2nd ed.: Zagreb, 1971-1974, 2 vols. ca. 2100 pp. Chief ed.: Krešimir Kovačević.
Encyclopedia of Music.   116

Plastic Arts

Enciklopedija likovnih umjetnosti. Zagreb, 1959-66, 4 vols., 2861 pp. Chief ed.: Andre Mohorovičić (vol. 1-3); Slavko Batušić, Andre Mohorovičić, Mirko Šeper (vol. 4).
Encyclopedia of sculpture, painting, engraving.   117

Mihačević, Borislav. *Mali rječnik likovnih umjetnosti*. Sarajevo, Narodna Prosvjeta, 1958, 90+iii pp.
Dictionary of plastic arts.   118

GEOGRAPHY and ECOLOGY

Baučić, Ivo et al. *Zemljopis — Školski leksikon*. Zagreb, Privreda, 1963, 251 pp.   119

Dizdarević, Muso. *Rječnik ekologije*. Sarajevo, Zavod za izdavanje udžbenika, 1974, 135 pp.   120

Roglić, Josip. *Prilog hrvatskoj krškoj terminologiji*. Zagreb, JAZU, 1974.   121

Šenoa, Milan. *Prilog za hrvatsku geografsku terminologiju.*
In: Nastavni vjesnik, knjiga IV, Zagreb 1896.   122

HISTORY

Saltzer, Olga. *Povijest — Školski leksikon.* Zagreb, Privreda,
1965, 188 pp.   123

LAW, ADMINISTRATION, POLITICS

Bogišić, Baltazar. *Stručno nazivlje u zakonima.* Spljet, 1876.
Technical terminology in laws.   124

Id. *Tehnički termini u zakonodavstvu.* Beograd, 1887, 18 pp.
Technical terms in legislature.   125

Hubeny, Marijan et al. *Međunarodni politički leksikon.* Zagreb,
1960, 592 pp.
Lexicon of International Politics.   126

Ibler, Vladimir. *Rječnik međunarodnog javnog prava.* Zagreb,
Informator, 1972, 386 pp.
Dictionary of International Public Law.   127

Kocian, S. *Tumač i rječnik zakonima o poreznoj reformi i
ostalim izravnim porezima.* I-IV, Zagreb, 1913.   128

Mažuranić, Vladimir. *Prinosi za hrvatski pravno-povjestni
rječnik.* Zagreb, 1908-22, XIX+1756 pp. Addenda 1923,
XV+74. Reprint: Zagreb, Informator, 1975, 2 vols.
Contributions to Croatian legal-historical lexicon.   129

Petranović, Božidar. *Ručna knjiga najnuždnijih pravdoslovnih
riečih, izriekah, i obraznicah.* Zadar, 1862, 124 pp.   130

Romac, Ante. *Rječnik rimskog prava.* Zagreb, Informator,
2nd ed. 1983, 480 pp.   131

LINGUISTICS

Babić, Stjepan. *Jezik*. Zagreb, Privreda, 1963, 146 pp. 2nd edition, Zagreb, Panorama, 1965, 322 pp. 3rd ed. Panorama, 1966, 322 pp. 4 ed. Panorama, 1967, 322 pp.
Linguistic terminology. 132

Maretić, Tomislav. *Pregled srpsko-hrvatske gramatičke terminologije XVII, XVIII i XIX vijeka*. In: Rad JAZU (243), Zagreb 1932.
Croatian grammatical terminology in the 17th, 18th and 19th centuries. 133

LITERATURE

Cubelić, Tvrtko. *Književni leksikon — Osnovni teorijsko-književni pojmovi i bio-bibliografske bilješke o piscima*. 3 ed. Zagreb, Tisak Riječke tiskare, 1972, LVI + 558 pp.
Dictionary of literary terms. 134

Taritaš, Milan. *Rječnik književne interpretacije*. Zagreb, Izdanje pisca, 1975, 160 pp.
Dictionary of literary interpretations. 135

MEDICINE, VETERINARY MEDICINE, PHARMACOLOGY, BIOLOGY

Babić, Ivo; Slavko Pavešić. *Terminologija veterinarske i humanomedicinske parazitologije*. Zagreb, JAZU, 1960, 134 pp.
Terminology of veterinary and medical parasitology. 136

Chudoba, Dinko. *Osnovna medicinska terminologija. Za početnike u struci i laike*. Zagreb, Naklada St. Kugli, 1937, 142 pp.
Basic medical terminology. 137

Dežman, Ivan. *Rěčnik lěčničkog nazivlja.* Zagreb, 1868, V +
1 + 1 + 141 pp. (in two columns).
Dictionary of medical terminology. 138

Fleischer, Gustav. *Rječnik narodnih imena ljekarija.* Bjelovar,
1893, 33 pp. (in two columns).
Dictionary of popular medical terms. 139

Glück, Leopold. *Medizinische Volksterminologie in Bosnien
und der Herzegovina.* Sarajevo, 1898.
Medical popular terminology in Bosnia and Herzegovina. 140

Građa za medicinsku terminologiju. In Liječnički Vjesnik,
1939-41.
Material for medical terminology. 141

Kuzmanić, Ante. *Ričnik likarskog nazivlja.* Zadar, 1875.
Dictionary of medical terms. 142

Leksikon zdravlja. Zagreb-Beograd, Minerva, 1936, 4 + 962
columns. Ed. Dr. Dragoljub Sretanović.
Lexicon of Health. 143

Leksikon zdravlja. Zagreb, Minerva, 1937, 4 + 938 columns.
Ed. Dr. Edo Deutsch.
Lexicon of Health. 144

Mayerhofer, Ernest; Miroslav Simončić. *Leksikon prehrane.*
Zagreb, HIBZ, 1944, 531 pp.
Lexicon of nutrition. 145

Medicinska enciklopedija. 1 ed.: Zagreb, 1957-74. 10 vols + 1.
Chief ed. Ante Šercer; 2 ed: Zagreb, 1967-70, 6 vols. 4200 pp.
Chief ed. Ante Šercer (vol. 1-4), Mirko Dražen Grmek (vol.
5-6). *Dopunski svezak Medicinske enciklopedije*, 1 vol. 768 pp.
(complementary vol. of Encyclopedia of Medicine). 146

Popularni medicinski leksikon. Zagreb, NIP, 1954, 1194 pp. 2nd ed. 1955, 1284 pp. 3rd ed. 1956, 1386 pp. Ed. Đ. Vukadinović.

Popular lexicon of medicine. 147

Prpić, Tomislav. *Rječnik starokajkavskog medicinskog nazivlja.* Zagreb, KUD Šandor K. Đalski, 1974, 23 pp.

Old Kajkavic medical terminology. 148

Seunig, Vera; Radovan Domac. *Biologija.* Zagreb, Privreda, 1963.

Terminology of biology. 149

Šercer, Ante. *Otorinolaringologija.* Zagreb, 1965-66, 2 vols. 1335 pp.

Encyclopedia of Otolaryngology. 150

Wirth, David. *Veterinarski leksikon za praktičnu terapiju i profilaksu.* Zagreb, Poljoprivredni nakladni zavod, 1952-53, Vol. I (A-N), Vol. II (O-Ž), 1278 pp.

Practical veterinary lexicon of therapeutics and pro-phylaxis. 151

PEDAGOGY, PHYLOSOPHY, PSYCHOLOGY, SOCIOLOGY

Basariček, Stjepan et al. *Pedagogijska enciklopedija.* Zagreb, Hrvatski pedagoško-književni zbor, 1895-1906, Vol. I (1-12 fascicles); Zagreb, 1908-1916, Vol. II (13-16 fascicles).

Encyclopedia of pedagogy. 152

Bosanac, Milan; Oleg Mandić, Stanko Petković. *Rječnik sociologije i socijalne psihologije.* Zagreb, Informator, 1977, 724 pp.

Dictionary of sociology. 153

Cudina, Mira; Josip Obradović. *Psihologija — Školski leksikon.* Zagreb, Privreda, 1963, 108 pp. 2nd ed. Zagreb, Panorama, 1965, 303 pp. 3rd ed. Panorama, 1967, 303 pp. 154

Filipović, Vladimir et al. *Filozofijski rječnik*. Zagreb, Matica hrvatska, 1965, 438 pp. 2nd ed. Zagreb, Matica hrvatska, 1984.
Dictionary of philosophy. Ca. 3000 philosophical concepts.   155

Franković, Dragutin; Zlatko Predrag. *Enciklopedijski rječnik pedagogije*. Zagreb, Matica hrvatska, 1963, 1146 pp.   156

Grlić, Danko. *Filozofija — Školski leksikon*. Zagreb, Privreda, 1963, 160 pp. 2nd ed. Zagreb, Panorama, 1965, 299 pp.   157

Hudolin, Vladimir. *Psihijatrijsko-psihološki leksikon*. Zagreb, Privreda, 1963, 427 pp. 2nd ed. Zagreb, Panorama, 1968, 430 pp.
Lexicon of psychiatry and psychology.   158

Martić, Mirko; Ante Marušić. *Nauka o društvu — Školski leksikon*. Zagreb, Privreda, 1963, 165 pp.   159

Pataki, Stevan; M. Tkalčić et al. *Pedagogijski leksikon*. Zagreb, Minerva Knjižara, 1939, 417 pp.
Lexicon of pedagogy.   160

RELIGION

Biblijski leksikon. Zagreb, Kršćanska Sadašnjost, 1972, 374 pp.
Biblical lexicon.   161

Dufour, Xavier Léon. *Rječnik biblijske teologije*. Zagreb, Kršćanska Sadašnjost, 1969, XXV+1582+30 pp.   162

Leksikon ikonografije, liturgike i simbolike zapadnog kršćanstva. Zagreb, Liber, 1979, 621 pp. Ed. Anđelko Badurina.
Lexicon of liturgical and symbolical iconography of Western Christianity.   163

53

Mandić, Oleg. *Leksikon Judaizma i Kršćanstva*. Matica hrvatska, 1969, 526 pp.   164

Šetka, Jeronim. *Hrvatska kršćanska terminologija*. Split, Marija, 1976, 366 pp.
Croatian Christian terminology of Greek, Latin and Slavonic origin.   165

SCIENCE, TECHNICS, TECHONOLOGY, CRAFTS

Belović-Bernadzikowska, Jelica. *Gragja za tehnološki rječnik ženskog ručnog rada*. Sarajevo, 1898-1906, V+444+196 pp. in two columns.
Needlework and fashion terminology.   166

Bordukalo, Bogdan; Thomas Roth. *Mali terminološki rječnik*. Zagreb, Zavod za primjenu elektroničkih računala i ekonomski inženjering, Centar za stručno osposobljavanje kadrova za automatsku obradu podataka, 1978, 151 pp.   167

Deželić, Mladen. *O hrvatskoj kemijskoj terminologiji*. In Nastavni Vjesnik, Knj. 49, 1940.   168

Freudenreich, Aleksandar. *Kako narod gradi na području Hrvatske*. Zagreb, 1972, 344 pp.
Contains a glossary of popular building terminology (pp. 275-330).   169

Hefele, Ferdo. *Opančar i opančarija — Građa za obrtno nazivoslovje*. 2nd ed. Zagreb, 1890.
Material for handicraft terminology (strapped softsoled footwear).   170

Id. *Naši domaći obrti — Građa za obrtno nazivoslovje*. Sisak, 1896.
Handicraft terminology.   171

Isaković, Alija. *Rječnik stare rudarsko-geološke terminologije*. Sarajevo, Oslobođenje, 1970, 119 pp.
Dictionary of mining and geological terminology. 172

Iveković, Hrvoje. *Unificirana jugoslavenska nomenklatura anorganske kemije*. Zagreb, Školska knjiga, 1966, 94 pp. 173

Ivezić, Stjepan. *Fizikalni rječnik*. Pula, Narodna tehnika, Savez za tehnički odgoj, Kotarski odbor, 1959, 567 pp. 174

Jugoslavenska tehnička terminologija. Elektrotehnika. Instalacioni materijal. Zagreb, 1931. Ed. Društvo jugoslavenskih inžinjera i arhitekata.
Electrotechnical terminology. 175

Kovač, B. *Strojarska terminologija. S ilustracijama. Elementi strojeva*. In Strojarstvo, Zagreb, 1968, No 9-10; 1970 No 1-6. 176

Laćan, M. *Nomenklatura organske kemije*. In Kemija u industriji (17), 1968, No 227, 289, 389.
Nomenclature of organic chemistry. |177

Neidhart, Nikola. *Geodetska terminologija*. In Geodetski list, Zagreb, 1949-1981.
Terminology of geodesy. 178

Perić, Miljenko. *Mali fotorječnik*. Zagreb, Fotokemika, 1961, 60 pp.
Dictionary of photography. 179

Ranogajac, Irena. *Nomenklatura organskih spojeva*. RU »Đuro Đaković«, Sarajevo, 1965, IV+130 pp. 180

Riedl, Viktor; Maks Plotnikov. *Fotorječnik*. Zagreb, Nakladni zavod Hrvatske, 1946, 217 pp.
Dictionary of photography. 181

Smrkić, Zlatko. *Uvod u televiziju.* Zagreb, Tehnička knjiga, 1968, 430 pp.

Contains a glossary of 650 television terms. 182

Stručna terminologija. In Elektrotehnika. Zagreb XII (1969), No 2. 183

Tehnička enciklopedija. 10 vols. Zagreb, Vol. 1 (1963), Vol. 2 (1966), Vol. 3 (1969), Vol. 4 (1973), Vol. 5 (1976), Vol. 6 (1979), Vol. 7 (1980), Vol. 8 (1982), Vol. 9 (1984).

Encyclopedia of technical sciences and technology. 184

Tonković, Kruno. *Mostovi.* Zagreb, Liber, 1981,325 pp.

Contains terminology concerning bridge building (30 pp.). 185

Velimirović, Mihajlo. *Ilustrirani leksikon tehničkih znanja.* Zagreb, Panorama, 1965, 734 pp, 2nd ed. 1965, 734 pp. 3rd ed. 1967, 734 pp. 4 ed. 1968, 734 pp. 186

Id. *Fizika — Školski leksikon.* Zagreb, Privreda, 1963, 181 pp. 187

Id. *Kemija — Školski leksikon.* Zagreb, Privreda, 1963, 183 pp. 188

Esih, Vinko. *Pomodni rječnik.* Zagreb, 1954, 66 pp.

Fashion (embroidery and millinery). 189

SEA, SHIPPING, FISHING

Građa za pomorsku terminologiju. In Anali Leksikografskog Zavoda, Zagreb, 1955, 244 pp.

Material for nautical terminology. 190

Haramina, E. *Leksikon lova i ribolova.* Zagreb, Panorama, 1964. 191

Jurišić, Blaž. *Pomorski nazivi u Vitezovićevu rječniku*. In Anali Jadranskog instituta JAZU, 1956.
Nautical terms in Vitezović's Dictionary.   192

Lulić, Boško. *Mali pomorski rječnik sa nazivima važnijih morskih riba*. Split, 1938.
A small nautical dictionary with the names of more important sea fish.   193

Kasumović, D. *Hrvatski pomorsko-tehnički nazivi*. In Tršćanski Lloyd; mjesečni prilog za pomorstvo u našem jeziku, počev od 1905.
Croatian nautical and technical terms in monthly supplement to Lloyd Triestino from 1905 onwards.   194

Majcen, G.; B. Siminiati. *Pomorski rječnik*. In Pomorstvo 2 (1947) No 2, 3, 4, 5, 6, 7, 8, 9, 10; 3 (1948) No 1.   195
Nautical glossary.

Mikoč, Jakov Anton. *Rěčnik rukokretni*. Rijeka, 1852, 353 pp. In manuscript, preserved in Zagreb University Library.
Dictionary of nautical terms.   196

Pomorska enciklopedija. Zagreb, 1954-64, 8 vols. 2nd ed: Zagreb, 1972-75, 6 vols, ca. 4200 pp. Chief ed.: Mate Ujević.
Maritime encyclopedia. A general Croatian encyclopedia useful for its biographies of notable Croats.   197

Skok, Petar. *Naša · pomorska i ribarska terminologija na Jadranu*. Split, 1933.
Nautical and fishing terminology along Adriatic Coast.   198

Vidović, Radovan. *Pomorska terminologija i pomorske tradicije*. In Čakavska Rič 7 (1977/8), pp. 99-156.
Nautical terminology.   199

Id. *Pomorski rječnik slavenske obale Jadrana.* Split, Logos, 1984, 590 pp.
   Nautical dictionary. Contains ca. 4150 head words, 350 of which are Latin. The Croatian section of the work is a dictionary of the nautical terms used along the Adriatic coast, from Istria to Boka Kotorska. The oldest maritime expressions originating in the Middle Ages can be found in the dictionary as can be words from Marulić's time, that is, from the 15th century, right up until the end of the sailing ship era and up until the time of today's sand dredges. 200

SPORT

Enciklopedija fizičke kulture. Zagreb, 1975-1977, 2 vols., 1450 pp. Chief ed. Marijan Flander.
   Encyclopedia of physical culture and sports. 201

Sportski leksikon. Zagreb, Leksikografski zavod 'M. Krleža', 1984. 202

THEATRE

Cindrić, Pavao. *Kazališna terminologija.* In Enciklopedija Hrvatskog Narodnog kazališta u Zagrebu, 1894-1969. Zagreb, 1969, 721 pp. (pp. 410-422). 203

ZOOLOGY, BOTANY

Boranić, Dragutin. *Zoološka terminologija i nomenklatura.* Zagreb, 1932.
   Zoological terminology and nomenclature. 204

Id. *Botanička terminologija.* Zagreb, 1934.
   Botanical terminology. 205

Domac, Radovan. *Flora. Za određivanje i upoznavanje bilja (po biljnoj sistematici)*. Zagreb, Izdavački zavod JAZU, 1950, 552 pp.   206

Fink, Nikola. *Imenik znanstvenih naziva životinja obrađenih u "Rječniku narodnih zoologičkih naziva"* M. Hirtza. Zagreb, JAZU, 1956, 50 pp.   207

Haračić, A. *Prilog za narodnu botaničku nomenklaturu*. In Glasnik Hrvatskog naravoslovnog društva, 1894.
Contribution to popular botanical nomenclature.   208

Hirtz, Miroslav. *Rječnik narodnih zoologičkih naziva, I Dvoživci (amphibia) i gmazovi (reptilia)*. Zagreb, JAZU, 1928, XV+197 pp.   209

Id. *Rječnik narodnih zoologičkih naziva, II Ptice (Aves)*. JAZU, 1938-47, 433 and 599 pp.   210

Hirtz, Miroslav; Nikola Fink. *Rječnik narodnih zooloških naziva, III Ribe (Pisces)*. JAZU, 1956, 478 pp.
Dictionary of popular zoological terms.   211

Hirtz, Miroslav. *Rječnik peradarstva*. Beograd, 1934.
Dictionary of poultry breeding.   212

Horvatić, Stjepan. *Ilustrirani bilinar*. Zagreb, Školska Knjiga, 1954, 768 pp.
Illustrated herbalist.   213

Kolombatović, Juro. *Zoološka terminologija. Godišnje izvješće realke*. Split, 1880-90.
Zoological terminology.   214

Id. *Imenik kraliešnika Dalmacije*. Split, 1885-86. Vol. 1 *Sisavci i ptice*, 38 pp. Vol. 2 *Dvoživci, gmazovi i ribe*, 32 pp.   215

Kosić, Baldo. *Ribe dubrovačke*. In Rad JAZU, (155) 1903.
Fish in Dubrovnik.   216

Id. *Dodatak raspravi "Ribe dubrovačke"*. Ibid. (158) 1904. 217

Kurelac, Fran. *Imena vlastita i splošna domaćih životin u Hrvatov a ponekle i Srbalj*. Zagreb, 1867, 64 pp. 218

Prohaska, Ljudevit. *Stočarska terminologija*. In Veterinarski Vjesnik, 1917, 2-12.
Terminology of cattle breeding. 219

Schlosser Klekovski; Josip Kalasancij; Ljudevit Vukotinović. *Flora croatica*. Zagreb, JAZU, 1869, CXLI+1362 pp. 220

Id. *Syllabus florae croaticae*. Zagreb, 1857, V+192+XVI pp. 221

Id. *Fauna kornjašah Trojedne Kraljevine*. Zagreb, JAZU, 1879, LVIII+995 pp. 222

Šoljan, Tonko. *Ribe Jadrana*. Split, Nakladni zavod Hrvatske, 1948 (1949), 437+3 pp. 223

Šulek, Bogoslav. *Jugoslavenski imenik bilja*. Zagreb, 1879, XXIII+564 pp. 224

Veseli, D. *Sistematika i nazivlje drveća i grmlja*. In Bosanski šumar, Sarajevo, 1929. 225

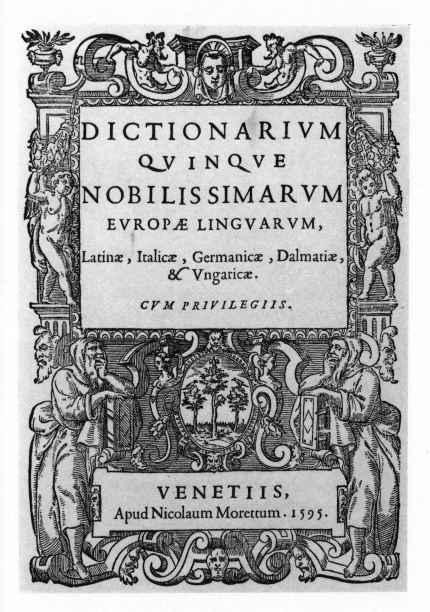

DICTIONARIVM
QVINQVE
NOBILISSIMARVM
EVROPÆ LINGVARVM,

Latinæ , Italicæ , Germanicæ , Dalmatiæ ,
& Vngaricæ.

CVM PRIVILEGIIS.

VENETIIS,
Apud Nicolaum Morettum . 1595.

The titlepage of Vrančić's *Dictionarium* . . . (Venice 1595)

BILINGUAL DICTIONARIES

ARABIC

Muftić, Teufik. *Arapsko-srpskohrvatski rječnik - Arapsko-hrvatskosrpski rječnik.* Sarajevo, Izvršni odbor Udruženja ilmije u SR B. i H., 1973, 2 vols. Vol. 1 XXVII+2019 pp. Vol. 2 2020-3950 pp.
    Arabic - Serbo-Croatian   226

Mujić, Muhamed. *Hrvatskosrpsko-arapski rječnik.*
    Ca. 50,000 words. (In manuscript.)
    Croatian-Arabic   227

CHINESE

Grujić, Branislav. *Srpskohrvatski-Kineski rječnik.* Cetinje, Obod, 1978, 700 pp.
    Ca. 30,000 words. Serbo-Croatian-Chinese   228

CZECH

Jelčić, A. *Slovník chorvatsko-srbsko-český.* Brno, 1914, 262 pp.
    Croatian-Serbian-Czech   229

Kadlec, J. *Česko-srbo-chorvatský.* Praha, s. a.
    Czech-Serbian-Croatian   230

Kout, Rudolf. *Nový kapesní slovník srbochorvatský a průvodce po jazyku srbohorvatském.* Třebíč, 1910, 438 pp. 2 ed: Třebíč, 1913, 37 pp. 430 columns. 3. ed: Trebič, 1913, 436 col. Other ed: Třebíč, 1925, 37 pp, 476 col.
    Serbo-Croatian-Czech   231

Mayer, Anton. *Slovníček česko-chorvatský.* Praha, 1912, 29 pp.
    Czech-Croatian   232

Merkhaut, Jaroslav. *Veliki češko-hrvatski rječnik*. *Česko-chorvatský slovník*. Zagreb, 1941, 596 pp. port.
Czech-Croatian 233

Noha, Miloš. *Srbocharvátsko-český a česko-srbocharvatský kapesní slovník*. Praha Státní Pedagogické Nakladatelství, 1961, 800 pp. 2 ed: 1965, 725 pp. 3 ed: Praha, SPN, 1967, 725 pp. 4 ed: Praha, SPN, 1967, 725 pp.
Czech-Serbo-Croatian
Serbo-Croatian-Czech 234

Očenášek, Jindřich. *Slovníček srbsko-neboli chorvatsko-český*. Praha, Otto, 1906, 58 pp.
Serbian or Croatian - Czech 235

Radić, Stjepan. *Rječnik češkoga jezika za Hrvate*. Zagreb, 1896, XVIII+104 pp.
Czech-Croatian 236

Radić, Stjepan. *Česko-hrvatska slovnica s čitankom i s česko-hrvatskim diferencijalnim rječnikom*. Zagreb, 1902, 2+147 pp.
Czech-Croatian 237

Sobotka, Otto. *Slovník Chorvatosrbsko-Český*. Daruvar, Jednota, 1973, 767 pp.
Croatian-Czech 238

Togner, V. *Kapesni slovník srbochorvatsko-český a česko-srbochorvatský*. Praha, 1939, 212, 214; 480 pp.
Czech-Serbo-Croatian
Serbo-Croatian-Czech 239

Special

Bilek, Miroslav. *Srbochorvatsko-český terminologický slovníček z matematiky a geometrie*. Praha, Československý Svaz LRCH, 1963, 22 leaves.
Croatian-Czech 240

Daněk, Alois. *Srbochorvatsko-český terminologický slovníček z poznáváni prírody a biologie.* Daruvar, Československý Svaz LRCH, 1962, 71 pp.

Kolouch, Otokar. *Srbochorvatsko-český terminologický slovníček zemepisu. Srpskohrvatsko-češki terminološki rječnik iz zemljopisa.* Praha, Československý Svaz v LRCH, 1963, 24 pp.

Milde, Václav. *Srbochorvatsko-český terminologický slovníček z dejepisu. Srpskohrvatsko-češki terminološki rječnik iz povijesti.* Praha, Československý Svaz v LRCH, 1963, 48 pp.

Sakař, Otokar. *Srbochorvatsko-český terminologický slovníček z technické výchovy.* Daruvar, Československý Svaz v RS Chorvatsku, 1963, 63 leaves.

ENGLISH

Andrović, Ivan. *New pronouncing and explanatory English-Croatian and Croatian-English dictionary, with typical phrases on every day topics.* 2 rev. ed. Zagreb, Mudrost, 1947 XXXVIII, 352 pp.

Bogadek, Francis Aloysius. *English-Croatian dictionary with correct pronunciation and appendix of special dictionary of birds, animals, fishes, reptiles, insects and worms, minerals, grain, green and vegetables, trees, fruits and flowers . . .* Pittsburgh, Marohnich, 1915, 750 pp.

Id. *New English-Croatian and Croatian-English Dictionary.*
Novi englesko-hrvatski i hrvatsko-engleski rječnik. New York,
1926. 2 enl. rev. ed: New York, Stechert, 1944, VII+531,
497, 46 pp. 3 enl.rev. ed: New York, Hafner, 1949, London,
Allen-Unwin, 1950, VII+531, 497, 46, 8 pp.
Contains a list of personal and geographical names
Croatian-English
English-Croatian   247

Id. *Najveći hrvatsko-engleski i englesko-hrvatski rječnik.*
Pittsburgh, Marohnich, 1917, 288, 206, 71 pp.
Croatian-English
English-Croatian   248

Brozović, Blanka; Oktavija Gerčan. *Englesko-hrvatski i hrvat-*
sko-engleski džepni rječnik za osnovnu školu. Zagreb, Školska
Knjiga, 1971, 252 pp. 2 ed. ŠK, 1973, 251 pp. 3 ed. ŠK, 251 pp.
English-Croatian
Croatian-English   249

Brozović, Stjepko. *Gramatika hrvatsko-englezka; razgovori*
za sve prilike života i englezko-hrvatski te hrvatsko-englezki
riečnik. New York, Narodni List, 1914, 434, 11 pp.
Croatian-English
English-Croatian   250

Bujas, Sunita; Zvonka Filipović. *Langenscheidtov Univerzalni*
Rječnik. English-Croatian. Hrvatsko-Engleski. Zagreb, Mla-
dost, 1971, XV+565 pp. 2 ed. 1977. 3 ed. 1978.
English-Croatian
Croatian-English   251

Bujas, Željko. *Hrvatski ili srpsko-engleski enciklopedijski*
rječnik. Zagreb, Grafički zavod Hrvatske, 1983, Vol. I (A-Lj),
665 pp.
Croatian-English   252

Drvodelić, Milan. *English-Croatian Dictionary*. Zagreb, Kugli, 1946. 253

Id. *Dictionary of the English and Croatian languages. Englesko-hrvatski i hrvatsko engleski rječnik.* Zagreb, Školska Knjiga, 1953-54, 940, 976 pp. 254

Id. *Hrvatsko ili srpsko - engleski rječnik.* 4 ed. Zagreb, Školska Knjiga, 1978, VIII+848 pp.
Croatian-English. 255

Id. *English-Croato-Serbian Dictionary and Croato-Serbian-English Dictionary. Englesko-hrvatsko-srpski, Hrvatsko-srpsko-engleski rječnik.* Zagreb, Školska Knjiga, 1961-62, 1,104, 912 pp.
English-Croatian-Serbian and Croatian-Serbian-English. In each case, about 35,000 headwords, including proper names 256

Id. *Hrvatsko-srpsko-engleski rječnik.* Zagreb, Školska Knjiga, 1961, 2 ed. Zagreb VII+912 pp. 257

Id. *Hrvatsko-srpsko-engleski i englesko-hrvatsko-srpski rječnik.* 3 ed. Zagreb, Školska Knjiga, 1970, 1,198, 913 pp.
English-Croatian-Serbian 258

Id. *Englesko-hrvatski ili srpski rječnik.* 4 ed. Zagreb, Školska Knjiga, 1973, VIII+1198. 5 ed. Zagreb, 1978. 6 ed. Zagreb, 1981, 880 pp. 7 ed. 1983. 259

Filipović, Rudolf; Berislav Grgić et al. *English-Croatian Dictionary. Englesko-hrvatski rječnik.* Zagreb, Zora, 1955, XVII+1430 pp. 2 enl. ed. Zagreb, Zora, 1961, ca. 100,000 words. 3 ed. Zagreb, Zora, 1963, XXI+1464 pp. 4 ed. (*Englesko-hrvatsko-srpski rječnik. Eglish-Croato-Serbian dictionary*). Zagreb, Zora, 1966, XXI+1468 pp. 5 ed. Zagreb, Zora, 1970, XXI+1468 pp. 10 ed. Školska Knjiga, 1980, XIX+1435 pp.
English-Croatian. 260

Jagrović, Dragan M. *Hrvatsko-englezka teoretsko-praktična gramatika i englezko-hrvatski te hrvatsko-englezki riečnik.* New York, F. Zetti, 1906, 272 pp.
English-Croatian
Croatian-English 261

Janković, Andro C. *Hrvatsko-englezki razgovori i riečnik. Croatian-English Dialogue and Dictionary.* 2 ed. Allegheny, Pa, Marohnich, 1903, 294 pp.
Croatian-English 262

Lochmer, Šandor. *Džepni rječnik hrvatskoga i engleskoga jezika sa točnim izgovorom svake riječi.* Zagreb, Hartman, 1911, 230 pp.
Croatian-English 263

Id. *Engleski učitelj; džepni rječnik za Srbe i Hrvate, sa točnim izgovorom svake riječi.* Chicago, Palandech, 19.., 195 pp. Other ed. Milwaukee, Caspar, 1917, under the title *English Instructor; or Croatian-English Pocket Dictionary*, 195 pp.
Croatian-English 264

Id. *Englesko-hrvatski rječnik. English-Croatian Dictionary.* Senj, Hreljanović, 1895 & 1906, 1112 pp.
English-Croatian 265

Id. (Lochmer, Aleksander). *Laki način engleski bez učitelja u kratko vrijeme naučiti, razumijevati i govoriti. Vježbe, razgovori i hrvatsko-engleski rječnik sa točnim izgovorom svake riječi.* 2 rev. ed. Chicago, Zagar, 1926, 171 pp.
Croatian-English 266

Petrović, Josip. *Hrvatsko-engleski, englesko-hrvatski rječnik.* Zagreb, Tehnička Knjiga, 1953, 262 pp.
Croatian-English
English-Croatian 267

Sikočan, Ivan. *Hrvat u Americi: Hrvatsko-engleski rječnik i besjedovnica.* St. Louis, By the author, 1911.
Croatian - English

Special

Bartolić, Ljerka. *Engineering English and its terminology. Tehnički engleski i njegova terminologija.* Zagreb, Školska Knjiga, 1962, 244 pp. 2 ed. 1966. 3 ed. 1971. 4 ed. 1976. 5 ed. 1979.
Contains a Croatian-English dictionary

Id. *Englesko-hrvatski ili srpski i hrvatsko ili srpsko-engleski rječnik brodograđevnih, strojarskih i nuklearno-tehničkih naziva.* Zagreb, Školska Knjiga, 1979, XII+276 pp.
English-Croatian
Croatian-English

Bubić, Šefkija. *Englesko-srpsko-hrvatski ekonomski rječnik. An English-Serbo-Croatian dictionary of economic terms.* Sarajevo, Veselin Masleša, 1959, 1040 pp.
English-Serbo-Croatian

Dragojlović, Pavle. *Informatika.* Zagreb, Školska Knjiga, 1971, 156 pp.
Contains an English-Croatian glossary of information theory

Filipović, Rudolf. *The Phonemic Analysis of English Loan-Words in Croatian.* Zagreb, 1960, 137 pp.

Hammel, Eugene A. *Serbo-Croatian Kinship Terminology.* (Kroeber Anthropological Society. Papers, no. 16, p. 45-75), Berkley, Calif., 1957.
Serbo-Croatian - English
Highlights differences in Serbian and Croatian usage. An appendix lists the alternative forms.

Ivir, Vladimir. *Hrvatsko ili srpsko-engleski rječnik privrednog nazivlja.* Zagreb, Školska Knjiga, 1978, 80 pp.
Croatian-English (economy)   275

Kulier, Ignac. *Englesko-hrvatski ili srpski prehrambeni rječnik.* Zagreb, Grafički zavod Hrvatske, 1980, 440 pp.
English-Croatian glossary of dietetics   276

Lazić, Svetislav, A. *Englesko-hrvatsko-srpski naftni rječnik.* Zagreb, Poslovno udruženje 'Nafta', 1976, 444 pp. 2 ed. 1978.
English-Croatian glossary of petroleum   277

Permanent Committee on Geographical Names glossaries. London, Royal Geographical Society, 1942-45.
Croatian   278

Ritz, Josip. *Englesko-hrvatskosrpski, hrvatskosrpsko-engleski poljoprivredni rječnik. English-Croatoserbian, Croatoserbian-English Agricultural Dictionary.* Zagreb, Sveučilište, 1969, IV+610 pp.   279

Short glossary for use on foreign maps; Serb and Croat. London, War Office, General Staff Geographical Section, 1943, 11 pp.
Serbian-Croatian - English   280

Short glossary of Serb and Croat. Washington, U.S. Army Map Service, 1943, 11 pp.   281

Spalatin, Leonardo. *Englesko-Hrvatskosrpski, Hrvatskosrpski-Engleski prirodoslovni rječnik s rječnikom izgovora.* Zagreb, Liber, 1980, 743 pp.
English-Croatian (terminology of natural sciences)
Croatian-English   282

Thompson, Anthony; Dana Čučković; Šime Jurić. *Rječnik bibliotekarskih stručnih izraza. Vocabularium bibliothecarii. Englesko-hrvatskosrpski. English-Croatoserbian.* Zagreb,

70

Školska Knjiga, 1965, 184 pp.
  English-Croatian (Dictionary of librarianship)
  Croatian-English   283

Urbani, Marijan. *Hrvatsko-engleski rječnik privredne terminologije.* Zagreb, Birozavod, 1961, 173 pp.
  Croatian-English (terminology of economy)   284

ESPERANTO

Bedeković, Danica. *Esperanto-hrvatski rječnik.* Zagreb, Društvo hrvatskih esperantista, 1909, VIII+294 pp. (in two columns).
  Esperanto-Croatian   285

Id. *Hrvatsko-esperantski rječnik.* Zagreb, Društvo hrvatskih esperantista, 1921, IV+93 pp. (in two columns).
  Croatian-Esperanto   286

Bubalo, Nikola. *Esperanto-hrvatskosrpski rječnik.* Zagreb, Društvo hrvatskih esperantista, 1923, 148 pp. (in two columns).
  Esperanto-Croatian   287

Gjivoje, Marinko. *Rječnik hrvatsko-srpsko-esperantski. Kroata-serba-esperanta vortaro.* Zagreb, Znanje, 1966, 369 pp.
  Croatian-Esperanto   288

Kraus, Lavoslav; Dragutin Wranka. *Esperanta vortaro.* 1952. 2 ed. 1953. 4 ed. Osijek, Esperanta Societo Liberiga Stelo, 1958, 84 pp.
  Esperanto-Croatian   289

Lisac, Nikola. *Esperanto-srpsko-hrvatski i hrvatsko-srpski-esperanto rječnik.* Sarajevo, 1934, 118 pp. (in 1-3 columns).
  Esperanto - Serbo-Croatian
  Croato-Serbian - Esperanto   290

Maruzzi, Dušan; Ivo Rotkvić. *Hrvatsko-srpski esperantski rječnik.* Zagreb, 1925, 133 pp. (in two columns).
Croatian-Esperanto

Vortareto esperanto kroata-serba por komencantoj kaj progresintoj. Osijek, 1935.
Esperanto-Croatian

FRENCH

Adamović, Julije. *Francusko-hrvatski rječnik s označenim izgovorom. Dictionnaire française-croate.* Zagreb, 1901, VIII+575+(1) pp. 2 rev. en. ed: Zagreb, 1921, VII+628 pp. 3 enl. ed: Zagreb, 1937, VIII+554 pp.
French-Croatian

Arhanić, Đuro; Viktor Živić. *Francusko-hrvatski rječnik.* Zagreb, 1937, VIII+946 pp.
French-Croatian

Batušić, Ivana et al. *Langenscheidtov Univerzalni Rječnik. Francusko-hrvatski rječnik.* Zagreb, Mladost, 1972, 549 pp.
French-Croatian

Dayre, Jean; Mirko Deanović; Rudolf Maixner. *Hrvatsko-srpsko-francuski rječnik. Dictionnaire croate ou serbe-français.* Zagreb, Novinarsko Izdavačko Poduzeće, 1956, XII+948 pp. 2 enl. ed:Zagreb, NIP, 1960, XVI+980 pp.
Croatian-French

Gavazzi, Artur. *Hrvatsko-francuski rječnik.* Zagreb, Župan, 1908, 8+444 pp. 2 ed. Zagreb, 1919, 6+444 pp. 3 ed: Zagreb, Kugli, 1933, 453 pp. (Rev. & ed. by Ferdinand Sarazin).
Croatian-French

Horetzky, Edita. *Francusko-hrvatski i hrvatsko-francuski džepni rječnik za osnovnu školu.* Zagreb, Školska Knjiga, 1972. 196 pp.
French-Croatian
Croatian-French 298

Maixner, Rudolf. *Dictionnaire de poche français-croatoserbe. Francusko-hrvatskosrpski džepni rječnik.* Zagreb, Školska Knjiga, 1962, VIII, XXIV+804 pp. 2 ed: Zagreb, Školska Knjiga, 1968, XII+812 pp.
French-Croatian
Croatian-French 299

Moguš, Milan et al. *Hrvatsko-francuski rječnik. Langenscheidtov džepni rječnik.* Zagreb, Mladost, 1981, IX+522 pp.
Croatian-French 300

Ninić, Dragica. *Rječnik za osnovne škole. Francusko-srpskohrvatski, srpskohrvatsko-francuski.* Sarajevo, Svjetlost, 1966, 116 pp.
French - Serbo-Croatian
Serbo-Croatian - French 301

Orešek. *A small Croatian-French glossary.* Second half of the 18th c. Contains ca 270 words. 302

Pierre, Paul. *Abrégé de dictionnaire français-croate.* Zagreb, 1869, 77+2 pp.
French-Croatian 303

Ploetz, Karl; Dragojla Lopašić. *Maleni rječnik najnužnijih rieči i razgovora francezkih. Petit vocabulaire français.* Karlovac, R. Reich, 1888. 2 ed. Zagreb, L. Hartman, 1906, 62+(2) pp. (in two columns). 304

Putanec, Valentin. *Francusko-hrvatskosprski rječnik*. Zagreb, Školska Knjiga, 1957, XV+957 pp. 2 enl. rev. ed. (Francusko-hrvatski ili srpski rječnik), Zagreb, 1973, XVI+976 pp. 3 enl. rev. ed: Zagreb, 1982, XX+1152 pp.
French-Croatian 305

Vinja, Vojmir. *Langenscheidtov Univerzalni Rječnik. Francusko-hrvatski, hrvatsko-francuski*. Zagreb, Mladost, 1971, 566 pp. 2 ed. 1978.
Croatian-French
French-Croatian 306

Special

Franolić, Branko. *Les Mots d'emprunt français en croate*. Paris, Nouvelles Editions Latines, 1976, XLII+216 pp.
French loanwords in Croatian 307

GERMAN

Božanović, Ana. *Rječnik za osnovne škole. Njemačko-srpsko-hrvatski i srpskohrvatsko-njemački*. Sarajevo, Svjetlost, 1966, 114 pp. 2 ed: Sarajevo, Svjetlost, 1970, 114 pp.
German - Serbo-Croatian 308

Esih, Vinko. *Njemačko-hrvatski i hrvatsko-njemački rječnik. Deutschkroatisches und kroatisch-deutsches Wörterbuch*. Zagreb, 1940-44, 558 pp.
Croatian - German
German - Croatian 309

Esih, Vinko; Ivan Esih. *Njemačko-hrvatski rječnik*. Zagreb, Naklada V. Esih, 1941-44, 2 vols. 862+558 pp.
German - Croatian 310

Filipović, Ivan. *Mali rječnik hrvatskoga i njemačkoga jezika.*
Zagreb, Hartman (I Njemačko-hrvatski dio), 4 ed. 1900, 3+532
pp (in two columns). 6 ed. 1906 (II Hrvatsko-njemački dio).
Croatian - German
German - Croatian   311

Filipović, Ivan; Gjuro Deželić; Ljudevit Modec. *Neues Wörter-*
buch der kroatischen und deutschen Sprache. Njemačko-
hrvatski (2 vols.), *Hrvatsko-njemački* (2 vols.) Zagreb, 1869-75,
4 vols. 2132, 796, 717 pp. 2 ed: Zagreb, 1877, 2132 pp. 4 ed.
Zagreb, Hartman, 1906, 552, 587 pp. 5 rev. enl. ed: Zagreb,
Hartman, 1910.
German - Croatian
Croatian - German   312

Filipović, Ivan. *Žepni rječnik hrvatskoga i njemačkoga jezika*
za porabu u školi i na putu. Zagreb, 1878. 2 ed. 1887. 3 ed.
1888, 4 ed. 1895. 5 ed. 1896. 6 ed. 1903.
Croatian - German   313

Fröhlich-Veselić, Rudolf Alois. *Ilirsko-njemački i njemačko-*
ilirski rukoslovnik. Beč, Lechner, 1839, 370, 400 pp.
Croatian - German
German - Croatian   314

Id. *Handwörterbuch der illirischen und deutschen Sprache.*
Rječnik ilirsko-njemački i njemačko-ilirski. Wien, Venedikt,
1853-54, VIII+570 pp; XVIII+776 pp.
Croatian-German
German-Croatian   315

Hauszer, Fabian. *Kroatisch-deutsches Wörterbuch für Schul-*
lehrer. Beč (Wien), 1858, 194 pp. Ca. 14,000 Croatian words.
Croatian-German   316

Hurm, Antun. *Njemačko-hrvatski rječnik s gramatičkim*
podacima i frazeologijom. Zagreb, Školska Knjiga, 1954, VIII
+697 pp. 5 ed. ŠK, 1978.
German - Croatian   317

75

Id. *Njemačko-hrvatskosrpski rječnik. Deutsch-kroato-serbisches Wörterbuch.* 2 ed: Zagreb, Školska Knjiga, 1959, 884 pp. 3 enl. ed: Zagreb, ŠK, 1968, XII+984.
German-Croatian 318

Id. *Njemačko-hrvatski ili srpski rječnik.* 4 ed: Zagreb, ŠK, 1974, XII+1024 pp. 5 rev. ed: Zagreb, ŠK, XII+804 pp.
German-Croatian 319

Id. *Hrvatsko-srpsko-njemački rječnik.* Zagreb, Školska Knjiga, 1959, 710 pp. 2 rev. enl. ed: Zagreb, ŠK, 1969, 818 pp.
Croatian-German 320

Id. *Hrvatskosrpsko-njemački rječnik s gramatičkim podacima i frazeologijom.* Zagreb, Školska Knjiga, 1958, 719 pp. 2 rev. ed. 1968, 820 pp. 3 ed. (*Hrvatsko ili srpsko-njemački rječnik*) Zagreb, 1973, 820 pp.
Croatian - German 321

Jambrešić, Andrija. *Index vocum croaticarum et germanicarum cum brevi introductione ad linguam croaticam.* Zagreb, 1738 (according to Šafařik)
Croatian (Kajkavic) - German 322

Id. *Nemške škole navuk, seu: Vocabularium croatico-germanicum.* Zagreb, 1765, Budapest, 1821 (according to Šafařik)
Croatian (Kajkavic) - German 323

Kleines Wörterbuch, deutsch und illyrisch. Beč (Wien), 1793 (according to Šafařik)
German - Croatian 324

Kleines kroatisches-deutsches Wörterbuch für die Jugend. Zagreb, F. Suppan, 1829, 48 pp.
Croatian - German 325

Kristijanović, Ignac. *Anhang zur Grammatik der Kroatischen Mundart.* Zagreb, 1840.
Contains Croatian (Kajkavic)-German & German-Croatian (Kajkavic) glossary 326

Krmpotić, Ivan. *Njemačko-hrvatski rječnik.* Zagreb, Naklada Knjižare Preporod, 1941, 2+520 pp.
German - Croatian 327

Lanosović, Marijan. *Neue Einleitung zur slavonischen Sprache.* Osijek, 1778. 2 ed. 1789. 3 ed. 1795. Contains *Slavonisches Wörterbuch*, pp. 121-200; 2 ed. 119-198.
Croatian - German 328

Mandrović, Konstantin. *Hrvatsko-njemački rječnik.* Beč - Leipzig, A. Hartleben's Verlag, 1943, 200 pp.
Croatian - German 329

Id. *Deutsch-Kroatisches Wörterbuch.* Wien - Leipzig, A. Hartleben's Verlag, 1943, 206 pp.
German - Croatian 330

Marak, Janko. *Hrvatsko-njemački rječnik.* Wien, Hartleben, Die Kunst der Polyglottie, Theil 65, 1900, 188 pp. 2 rev. ed: Wien, Hartleben, 1915, 187 pp. 3 ed: Wien, 1920.
Croatian - German 331

Id. *Deutsch-Kroatisches Wörterbuch.* Wien, Die Kunst der Polyglottie. Theil 68, 1901, 187 pp.
German - Croatian 332

Mayer, Anton. *Langenscheidtov Univerzalni Rječnik. Hrvatsko-srpsko-njemački. Njemačko-hrvatsko-srpski.* Zagreb, Mladost, 1964, 638 pp. Other ed: Zagreb, Mladost, 1969, 366 pp.
Croatian - German
German - Croatian 333

77

Id. *Universalwörterbuch. Serbokroatisch-Deutsch. Deutsch-Serbokroatisch.* Berlin, Langenscheidt, 1955, 364 pp. 3 ed: 1957
 Croatian - German
 German - Croatian   334

Mažuranić, Ivan; Jakov Užarević. *Njemačko-ilirski slovar. Deutsch-illyrisches Wörterbuch.* Zagreb, Gaj, 1842, 486 pp.
 German - Croatian   335

Medić, Ivo. *Njemačko-hrvatski i hrvatsko-njemački džepni rječnik za osnovnu školu.* Zagreb, Školska Knjiga, 1971. 2 ed. 1973. 3 ed. 1975, 228 pp. 4 rev. ed. 1977, 248 pp. 5 ed. 1979.
 German - Croatian
 Croatian - German   336

Německo-hèrvatski i hèrvatsko-německi rěčnik ... Beč, 1869, 99 pp.
 Croatian - German
 German - Croatian   337

Oehler, Heinz et al. *Grundwortschatz Deutsch-Serbokroatisch.* Stuttgart, 1974, 144 pp.
 German - Serbo-Croatian   338

Pavec, Ivan. *Njemačko-hrvatski rječnik za I i II dio Madeirinih njemačkih čitanaka.* Zagreb, Naklada Kr. hrvatsko-slav.-dalm. zemaljske vlade, 1877, 2+151 pp. (in two columns)
 German - Croatian   339

Reljković, Matija Antun. *Nimačko-ilirički i ilirićko-nimački ričnik. Deutsch-illyrisches und illyrisch-deutsches Wörterbuch.* Beč, 1796, 2 vols.
 Croatian - German
 German - Croatian   340

Id. *Slavonische und Deutsche Grammatik und Wörterbuch.*
2 ed: Wien, 1774
Croatian - German   341

Richter, Adolf Friedrich; Adolf Joseph Ballmann. *Ilirsko-němacski i němacsko-ilirski rukoslovnik.* *Illyrisch-deutsches und deutsch-illyrisches Handwörterbuch.* Wien, 1839-40, 2 vols.
Croatian - German
German - Croatian   342

Ryečnik malyi; das ist kleines Wörterbuch. Budim, 1806, 104 pp. Other ed: Budim, Univerzitet, 1823, 53 pp.
Croatian - German   343

Šamšalović, Gustav. *Njemačko-hrvatski i hrvatsko-njemački rječnik.* I *Njemačko-hrvatski dio.* II *Hrvatsko-njemački dio.*
Zagreb, Naklada knjižare Lj. Hartman, 1916, 316 pp.
German - Croatian
Croatian - German   344

Id. *Njemačko-hrvatsko-srpski i hrvatsko-srpsko-njemački rječnik.* Zagreb, Jugoslavenska Štampa, 1929, 661 , 729 pp.
Croatian - German
German - Croatian   345

Id. *Njemačko-hrvatski priručni rječnik.* 2 rev. ed: Zagreb, 1944, XV + 938 pp. Other ed: Zagreb, 1960, XI + 1291 pp.
German - Croatian   346

Id. *Njemačko-hrvatski rječnik.* *Deutsch-kroatisches Wörterbuch.* 2 ed: Zagreb, 1964, XV + 1201 pp. 3 ed: Zagreb, Zora, 1968, XI + 1201 pp. 4 ed: Zagreb, Zora, 1971, XI + 1201 pp. 7 ed. Grafički zavod Hrvatske, 1978.
German - Croatian   347

Scherzer, Ivan. *Praktični rječnik hrvatskoga-srpskoga i njemačkoga jezika. Njemački-hrvatski-srpski dio.* Beč, U Car-

skoj kraljevskoj nakladi školskih knjiga, 1908, 412 pp. *II. Hrvatsko-srpski-njemački dio.* Beč, 1909, 374 pp. 4 ed: Berlin, Verlag von Neufeld & Henius, 1915. Other ed: Osijek, Krbavac-Pavlović, 1925, 1937, 1942, VIII+314, 302 pp.
German - Croatian
Croatian - German   348

Id. *Njemački-hrvatski-srpski dio,* 2 ed. Beč, 1913, 412 pp.
German - Croatian   349

Sedlar, Antun. *Deutsch-Kroatisch.* Leipzig, F. Brandstetter, 1943, 52 pp.
German - Croatian   350

Sprachübungen in der deutschen und kroatischen Sprache nebst einem deutsch-kroatischen Wörterbuch. Karlovac, 1823 351

Škrobot, Ladislav. *Kleines illyrisch-deutsches Wörterbuch für die Jugend der Militaer-Grenzschulen.* Agram, Gaj, 1839, 45 pp.
Croatian - German   352

Šulek, Bogoslav. *Deutsch-kroatisches Wörterbuch. Rěčnik německo-hrvatski.* Zagreb, Zupan, 1854-60, 2 vols., VIII+ 1712 pp.
German - Croatian   353

Tadijanović, Blaž. *Svašta po malo.* Magdeburg, 1761, /24/+ 191 pp. 2 ed: Troppau, 1766, /26/+201 pp.
Conversational German-Croatian Dictionary   354

Tangl, Eberhard. *Kroatisches Taschenwörterbuch. Kroatisch -deutsch und Deutsch-kroatisch. Mit einem Anhang der Wichtigeren Neubildungen.* Berlin, Junckers Wörterbücher, 1941, 302, 314+32 pp. Other eds: Berlin, 1955, 302, 314, 32 pp; Berlin, 1958, 302, 314, 32 pp.
Croatian - German
German - Croatian   355

Vocabularium croatico-germanicum to jest nemške škole navuk kak Horvatom tak Nemcem na hasen. *Kroatisch-deutsches Wörterbuch bei der Nationen zum Unterricht.* Ofen, Kön. ung. Universitätsschriften, 1835, 32 pp. 2 ed. 1841, 32 pp.
    Croatian (Kajkavic) - German   356

Zahradnik, R.M. *Praktisches deutsch-kroatisches Notwörter-buch.* Sarajevo, 1902.   357

Special

Altman, Josip; Stevan Bukl et al. *Rječnik njemačko-hrvatskoga tehnologičkoga nazivlja.* Zagreb, C. Albrecht, 1881, 417 pp. Ca. 25,000 terms.
    German - Croatian (technical terminology)   358

Id. *Gradjevni pristojbenik to jest Pristojbenik za sve zanate zasjecajuće u gradjevnu struku.* Zagreb, Klub inžinira i arhi-tekta, 1882, 249 pp. 2 ed: Zagreb, 1904, 249 pp.
    Contains a Croatian-German glossary of building ter-minology (30 pp.)   359

Dabac, Vlatko. *Njemačko-hrvatski i hrvatsko-njemački elektro-tehnički rječnik. Deutsch-kroatisches und kroatisch-deutsches elektrotechnisches Wörterbuch.* Zagreb, Školska Knjiga, 1952, XV+356 pp.
    Croatian - German (ca. 10,500 Croatian terms)
    German - Croatian (ca. 7,000 German terms)   360

Id. *Tehnički rječnik. Dio I Njemačko-hrvatskosrpski. Techni-sches Wörterbuch. Deutsch-kroatoserbisch.* Zagreb, Tehnička Knjiga, 1969, XXX+1,104 pp. *Dio II Hrvatskosrpski-njemački.* Zagreb, 1970, XXXIV+1574 pp.
    German - Croatian
    Croatian - German   361

Depoli, Jakob. *Poštarski rečnjak složen azbučnim redom njemački i hrvatski.* Zagreb, 1871, 52 pp.
German - Croatian (dictionary of postal terms)   362

Esih, Vinko. *Jela i prilozi na hotelskom stolu. Gerichte und Beilagen auf dem Restaurantstische. Hrvatsko-njemački. Kroatsich-deutsch.* Karlovac, Vlastita naklada, 1957, 18 pp.
Croatian - German (catering terminology)   363

Filipović, Ivan. *Neues Wörterbuch der kroatischen und deutschen Sprache. Zum Gebrauche für Juristen, Beamte.* Zagreb, Lj. Hartman, 1869, 796 pp.
Croatian - German   364

Frleta, Rudolf. *Hrvatsko-njemački priručnik za ugostiteljske namještenike.* Zagreb, 1951, 48 pp.
Croatian - German (catering terminology)   365

Hajdenjak, A. *Njemačko-hrvatsko nazivlje pri proučavanju ženskoga ručnoga posla u pučkih i građanskih školah.* Zagreb, 1877.
German - Croatian (needlework terminology)   366

Hlava, Dragutin. *Njemačko-hrvatski šumarski rječnik.* 1873, 32 leaves; manuscript kept in Zagreb University Library (R. 6370)
German - Croatian (dictionary of forestry)   367

Peričić, Božo. *Medicinski rječnik njemačkoga i hrvatskoga jezika.* Zadar, Štamparija 'Narodnog lista', 1906, VII+130 pp.
German - Croatian (dictionary of medicine)   368

Id. *Medicinski rječnik hrvatskoga i njemačkoga jezika.* Zadar, Štampa H. pl. Schönfelda, 1919, 196 pp.
Croatian - German (dictionary of medicine)   369

GREEK
(Ancient and Modern)

Špehar, M. *Rječnik za vježbe sadržane u Schenklovoj grčkoj početnici za III i IV gimnazijski razred.* Zagreb, s.a. 377

Žepić, Milan; M. Krkljuš. *Grčko-hrvatski rječnik.* Zagreb, 1903, 946 pp.
Greek (Ancient) - Croatian 378

Special

Bedjanić, Martin. *Rječnik Homerovih pjesama.* Zagreb, Naklada spisateljeva, 1901, 2+290 pp.
Greek (Ancient) - Croatian 379

Kuzmić, Martin. *Slovnica i rječnik stručnih izraza iz grčkog jezika.* 1919, 248 leaves; manuscript kept in Zagreb University Library (R 4030) 380

Marn, Franjo. *Homerov rječnik za gimnazije.* Zagreb, Nakl. Kr. sveučilišne knjižare Franje Suppan, 1892, 130 pp.
Greek (Ancient) - Croatian 381

Vasmer, Max. *Die griechischen Lehnwörter im Serbokroatischen.* Pruessische Akademie der Wissenschaften. Phil.-Hist. Klasse, Abhandlungen, no. 3, 1944. Berlin, 1944, VI+154 pp.
Greek loan words in Serbo-Croatian 382

HUNGARIAN

Bojničić, Ivan. *Gramatika mađarskog jezika.* 4 ed. Zagreb, Lj. Hartman, 1912, 288 pp.
Contains Hungarian-Croatian dictionary, pp. 219-263, and Croatian-Hungarian dictionary, pp. 264-286 383

Hadrovics, László. *Magyar-szerbohorvát szótár.* Budapest, Terra, 1968, 655 pp, ca. 25,000 words.
Hungarian - Serbo-Croatian   384

Id. *Magyar-szerbhorvát & szerbhorvát-magyar szótár.* Budapest, Terra, 1957-58, 656, LXIV+688 pp.
Hungarian - Serbo-Croatian
Serbo-Croatian - Hungarian   385

Levasics, E.; M. Surányi. *Szerbhorvát-magyar kéziszótár.* Budapest, Terra, 1967, 848 pp, ca. 50,000 words.
Serbo-Croatian - Hungarian   386

Margalits, Ede. *Horvát-magyar és Magyar-horvát zsebszótár.* Budapest, Az Athenaeum irod. és nyomdai r. társulat kiadása, 1898, XI+145+188 pp.
Croatian - Hungarian
Hungarian - Croatian   387

Margitai, József. *Magyar-horvát, horvát-magyar rövid zsebszótár.* Nagy-Kanizsa, 1887-1888, 2 vols.
Hungarian - Croatian
Croatian - Hungarian   388

Palich, Emil. *Magyar-szerbhorvát kéziszótár.* Budapest, Terra, 1968, XXXVI+937 pp, ca. 45,000 words
Hungarian - Serbo-Croatian   389

Sándor, S. *Rječnik hrvatskog i mađarskog jezika, I Mađarsko-hrvatski; II Hrvatsko-mađarski.* Budimpešta, s. a.
Hungarian - Croatian
Croatian - Hungarian   390

Spicer, Mauro (Mór). *Magjarsko-hrvatski i hrvatsko-magjarski rječnik. Magyar-horvát és horvát-magyar szótár.* Budimpešta, Magj. lit. zavod i tiskara Društva Franklin, 1893, 411 pp.
Hungarian - Croatian
Croatian - Hungarian   391

Šarčević, Ambrozije (Sárcsevics Ambrus). *Magyar-Szerb-Horvát-Bunyevácz-Sokácz Könyvészeti Szótár.* Szabadka, 1894, 136 pp.

Special

Frenyó, Lajos. *Terminologija fizike za opće škole sa srpskohrvatskim nastavnim jezikom.* Budapest, Tankönyvkiadó, 1962, 15 pp.
Croatian - Hungarian

Id. *Terminologija kemije za opće škole sa srpsko-hrvatskim nastavnim jezikom.* Budapest, Tankönyvkiadó, 1962, 15 pp.
Croatian - Hungarian

Janiszewsky, Vladimir, *Magyar-horvát és horvát-magyar szótár az országos kataszteri felmérés használatára.* Budapest, Tankönyvkiadó, 1912.
Hungarian - Croatian
Croatian - Hungarian

Krunity, Dömötör. *Terminologija biologije za opće škole sa srpskohrvatskim nastavnim jezikom.* Budapest, Tankönyvkiadó, 1962, 71 pp.
Croatian - Hungarian

Szabó, Gyula. *Terminologija računa i geometrije za opće škole sa srpskohrvatskim nastavnim jezikom.* Budapest, Tankönyvkiadó, 1962, 31 pp.
Croatian - Hungarian

Šarčević, Ambrozije. *Magyar-délszláv közigazgatási és törvény kezési műszótár. Magyar-délszláv rész.* Szabadbán, Nyomatatt Bittermann Károly özvegyénél, 1870, VIII+226 pp.
Hungarian - South Slav political and Juridical dictionary

Tóth, Tividar; Dragutin Schweitzer; Šandor Pandić; Mavro Spicer. *Vojnički rječnik; Magjarsko-hrvatski, hrvatsko-magjarski. Katonai szótár; magyar-horvát, horvát-magyar.* Budapest, Pallas, 1900-03, 517, 574 pp.

Hungarian - Croatian
Croatian - Hungarian   399

ITALIAN

Andrović, Ivan. *Rječnik talijansko-hrvatski. Dizionario italiano-croato.* Zagreb, Naklada dr. Vinko Esih, 1938, XIV+1231; 2 ed. 1942, XIV+1231+45 pp. Other ed: Milano, Hoepli, 1943, 1944, 612, 704 pp. Milano, Hoepli, 1980.
Italian - Croatian   400

Cekinić, L. *Vocabolario italinano-illirico.* Ca. 1731-45, preserved in manuscript.   401

Deanović, Mirko. *Rječnik talijanskog i hrvatskog jezika. Vocabolario italiano-croato.* Zagreb, Kugli, 1942, 28+803 pp. Suppl. 1945, 24 pp. (with Josip Jernej). 2 rev. ed: Zagreb, Nakladni Zavod Hrvatske, 1948, XXXI+828 pp.
Italian - Croatian   402

Deanović, Mirko; Josip Jernej. *Džepni rječnik talijanskog i hrvatskog jezika.* Zagreb, St. Kugli, 1944, 291 pp.
Italian - Croatian   403

Id. *Hrvatsko-srpsko-talijanski rječnik. Vocabolario croato-serbo-italiano.* Zagreb, Školska Knjiga, 1956, XI + 1164 pp. 2 enl. ed: Zagreb, Školska Knjiga, 1963, XVI+1192 pp. 3 enl. ed: Zagreb, ŠK, 1970, XVI+1224 pp. 4 enl. ed: Zagreb, ŠK, 1975, XVI+988 pp.
Croatian - Italian   404

Id. *Talijansko-hrvatsko-srpski i Hrvatsko-srpsko-talijanski rječnik.* Zagreb, Školska Knjiga, 1960, 2082 pp.
Italian - Croatian
Croatian - Italian   405

Id. *Talijansko-hrvatsko-srpski rječnik. Vocabolario italiano croato-serbo.* 3 rev. enl. ed: Zagreb, Školska Knjiga, 1960, XIV, 916 pp. 4 ed: Zagreb ŠK, 1973, XII+787 pp. 5 ed: Zagreb, ŠK, 1980, XVI+976 pp.
Italian - Croatian   406

Dizionario croato-italiano (Hrvatsko-talijanski rječnik). Milano, Casa ed. Bieti, 1942, 574 pp.
Croatian - Italian   407

Dizionario italiano-croato. Milano, Casa ed. Bieti, 1942, 576 pp.
Italian - Croatian   408

Ercegović, V.; S. Vekarić. *Dizionario croato-italiano (Hrvatsko-talijanski rječnik).* Dubrovnik, 1941. 2 ed. 1947.
Croatian - Italian   409

Id. *Dizionario italiano-croato (Talijansko-hrvatski rječnik).* Dubrovnik, 1942.
Italian - Croatian   410

Esih, Ivan; Ante Velzek. *Talijansko-hrvatski rječnik.* Zagreb, Binoza, 1942, 286 pp.
Italian - Croatian   411

Id. *Hrvatsko-talijanski rječnik.* Zagreb, Binoza, 1941 & 1943, 239 pp.
Croatian - Italian   412

Esih, Vinko. *Hrvatsko-talijanski rječnik.* Zagreb, 1942.
Croatian - Italian   413

Garin, A.M. *Rječnik italijansko-srpskohrvatski i srpsko-hrvatsko-italijanski. Dizionario italiano-serbocroato e serbo-croato-italiano.* Sarajevo, Džepna Knjiga, 1956, 226 pp. Other ed. 1958.
Italian - Serbo-Croatian
Serbo-Croatian - Italian   414

Jernej, Josip. *Džepni talijansko-hrvatski rječnik.* Zagreb, 1944.
Croatian - Italian   415

Id. *Talijansko-hrvatski i hrvatsko-talijanski džepni rječnik.* Zagreb, Školska Knjiga, 1973, 405 pp.
Italian - Croatian
Croatian - Italian   416

Jernej, Ljerka; Branimir Jernej. *Langenscheidtov Univerzalni Rječnik. Talijanko-hrvatski; Hrvatsko-talijanski.* Zagreb, Mladost, 1975, 693 pp.
Italian - Croatian
Croatian - Italian   417

Jasenković, Abdulah; Mesud Branković. *Rječnik italijansko-srpskohrvatski i srpskohrvatsko-italijanski. Dizionario italiano-serbocroato e serbocroato-italiano.* 2 ed: Sarajevo, Džepna Knjiga, 1958, 332 pp.
Italian - Serbo-Croatian
Serbo-Croatian - Italian   418

Jurašić, I. *Dizionario italiano-illirico.* Trieste, Lloyd, 1863, VII+784 pp.
Italian - Croatian   419

Kašić, Bartol. Without a title (Croatian (Čakavic) - Italian dictionary). 17th c. manuscript preserved in the library of Minor Brethren in Dubrovnik   420

Klašić, Matija (Cliasci Matthaeus). *Vocabula italico-illyrica.*
First half of the 18th c. Manuscript is kept in the library of
Minor Brethren in Dubrovnik.
Italian - Croatian   421

Matijašević, Djuro. *Rječnik hrvatskog jezika istumačen talijan-
skim jezikom.* Ca. 1700, 151 leaves; manuscript is preserved
in Zagreb University Library (R 5200)
Croatian - Italian   422

Parčić, Dragutin Antun. *Riečnik ilirsko-talijanski.* Zadar,
Petar Abelić, 1858, XIV+847 pp. 2 ed: *Rječnik slovinsko-
talijanski.* Zadar, 1874, VIII+1059 pp. 3 ed: *Rječnik hrvatsko-
talijanski. Vocabolario croato-italiano.* Zara, Narodni List,
1901, XII+1237 pp.
Croatian - Italian   423

Id. *Rječnik talijansko-slovinski (hrvatski). Vocabolario italiano-
slavo (Croato).* Zadar, Battara, 1868, 1146 pp. 2 ed: Segna,
H. Luster, 1887, VIII+932+VIII pp. 3 ed: Senj, Hreljanović,
1908, X+932 pp.
Italian - Croatian   424

Pohl, Hans Dieter. *Das italienisch-kroatische Glossar MS
Selden Supra 95.* Edition des Textes und linguistischer Kom-
mentar, "Schriften der Balkankommission. Linguistische
Abteilung XXIV/1 Österreichische Akademie der Wissenschaften, Philosophisch-historische Klasse, Wien, 1976, pp.
1-124.
   16th c. Italian-Croatian glossary; preserved in ms. in
   the Bodleian Library at Oxford   425

Romizi, G. *Dizionario italiano-croato.* Rijeka, 1934.
Italian - Croatian   426

Sommaripa, Gregorio Alasia da. *Dittionario Italiano et Schiavo.*
Udine, 1603. Other ed: Videm, 1607; contains 2633 words.
Croatian - Italian   427

Sučić, Ivo. *Dizionario italiano-croato e croato-italiano.* Zagreb, Naklada Dubrava, 1941, 304 pp., 2 ed. s.a.
Italian - Croatian
Croatian - Italian   428

Šutina, Jerko. *Vocaboli di prima necessita e dialoghi familiari originali illirici con versione italiana, scritti a caratteri latini e serbiani aggiuntovi un compendio di grammatica illirica per vantaggio della gioventù studiosa.* Zara, Fratelli Battara, 1850, 204 pp.
1850, 204 pp. 2 ed: Zadar, Battara, 1855, 191 pp.
Croatian - Italian   429

Švrljuga, Ivan Krst. *Talijansko-hrvatski i hrvatsko-talijanski džepni rječnik. Dizionario tascabile croato-italiano e italiano-croato.* Zagreb, Hartman, 1904, 308, 393 pp. 3 ed. 1942.
Italian - Croatian
Croatian - Italian   430

Id. *Talijansko-hrvatski džepni rječnik.* Zagreb, L. Hartman, 1927, 309 pp.
Italian - Croatian   431

Tanzlingher, Giovanni. *Vocabulario Italiano ed Illirico.* Zara, 1699. Folio. Manuscript preserved in the British Museum Library (10, 360).
Croatian (Čakavic) - Italian   432

Tomić, A. *Parlo serbocroato. Manuale di conversazione con pronuncia figurata.* Milano, Antonio Vallardi, 1980, 206 + XVI.
Contains Italian-Croatian vocabulary, pp. 5-206   433

Urbani, Umberto. *Dizionario delle lingue italiana e croata.* Parte prima Italiano-croata. Parte seconda Croato-italiana. Trieste, 1944, VII + 325 pp.   434

Valentiano, Lupis. *Opera nuova che insegna a parlare la lingua schiavonesca alli grandi, alli picoli et alle donne.* Ancona?, 1527.

Croatian - Italian

Italian - Croatian 435

Zvanik novi, s kojim svaki od sebe samoga moći će pridobro naučiti razgovoriti latinski i hrvatski. Vocabolario nuovo con il quale ciascuno da se stesso potra benissimo imparare a parlar italiano in slavo. U Bnecih (Venice), 1737, 24 pp.

Croatian - Italian 436

Special

Babić, Božo. *Morski rječnik hrvacko-srpski. Usporedjen sa italijanskim jezikom.* Trst, Tisk. Appolonia i Kaprina, 1870, 17 pp.

A comparative Croatian-Italian glossary of nautical terms 437

Hyrkkänen, Jukka. *Der lexikalische Einfluss des Italianischen auf das Kroatische des 16. Jahrhunderts. Die italienischen Lehnwörter im Sprachgebrauch der dalmatischen Kroaten im Lichte der Kroatischen Renaissance-Literatur.* Helsinki, 1973, 637 pp. (Doctoral thesis in manuscript)

Italian loanwords in 16th century Croatian 438

Jernej, Josip. *Sugli italianismi penetrati nel serbo-croato negli ultimi cento anni.* Zagreb, Studia Romanica, I, 1956, 54-82. 439

Luppi, Aldo. *Talijansko-hrvatskosrpski rječnik poslovne terminologije. Dizionario tecnico-commerciale italiano-croato.* Zagreb, 1973, X+740 pp.

Italian - Croatian (commercial dictionary) 440

Vidov, Božidar. *Vocabolario in dialetto della località dell'*
isola linguistica croata nel Molise. Toronto, 1972, 96 pp.
182 columns, 2500 words.
Italian - Croatian
Croatian - Italian   441

LATIN

Alvarez, Manuel. *Grammaticae latinae partes III.* Zagrabiae,
Weitz, 1750. Contains: *Radices latinae linguae, rěčnik latino-*
horvatski, pp. 161-375
Latin - Croatian   442

Ars magna parvulorum ali Nacsin kratek horvatzke rechi na
diacske obracsati y pravo zkupa szlagati. Zagrabiae, Bartholomaei Pallas, 1724, 32 pp.
Croatian - Latin   443

Belloszténëcs, Joannes. *Gazophylacium seu latino-illyricorum*
onomatum aerarium, select. synonymis, phraseologiis, verb.
construct., metaphoris, adagiis ... et nunc primum peculiariter
Illyriorum commodo apertum. Zagrabiae, Johannes Baptista
Weitz, 1740. 14 pp + 5 leaves + 1288. *Gazophylacium illyrico-*
latinum. 650 pp. Reprint, Zagreb, Liber, 1972-73.
Latin - Croatian
Croatian - Latin   444

Divković, Mirko. *Rječnik hrvatsko-latinski.* Zagreb, Nakl.
Kr. hrvatsko-slav.-dalm. zemaljske vlade, 1877, 1 1.+20 pp.
Croatian - Latin   445

Id. *Latinsko-hrvatski rječnik.* Zagreb, 1900, VII+1161 pp. 2 ed:
1917; other ed.: Zagreb, ITRO Naprijed, 1981. Contains
25,000 entries.
Latin - Croatian   446

Doroghy, Zvonimir. *Latinsko-hrvatski džepni rječnik.* Zagreb, St. Kugli, 1943, 273 pp.
Latin - Croatian 447

Habdelić, Juraj. *Dictionarium Croatico-Latinum. Dictionar, ili Reči slovenske zvekšega vkup zebrane, v red postavljene i diačkemi zlahkotene.* Graz, 1670
Croatian (Kajkavic) - Latin 448

Jakobović, Matija. *Dikcionar, Ričnik hrvatsko-latinski.* 1710. Preserved in manuscript, kept in the archives of Franciscans on Visovac.
Croatian - Latin 449

Katić, Frano. *Srpskohrvatski-latinski rječnik.* Beč (Wien), Carska Kraljevska naklada školskih knjiga, 1904, III+494 pp.
Croatian - Latin 450

Kunić, Pilip. *Slovnica jezika latinskoga ilirski iztumačena za porabu mladeži bosanske s kratkim i potrebitim riečnikom.* Beč, Štampano kod oo. Mechitaristach, 1857, IV+169(1) pp.
Latin - Croatian 451

Matthaei, Georgius (Matij(aš)ević, Juraj). *Dictionarium latino-illyricum.* 1716. Manuscript kept in the library of the monastery of Minor Brethren in Dubrovnik. 452

Rečnik horvatsko-latinski. 18th c. 102 pp. Manuscript is kept in Zagreb University Library (R 3672) 453

Ritter-Vitezović, Pavao. *Lexicon latino-illyricum.* 1700-1709, 1132 pp. Manuscript is kept in Metropolitana, MR 112, Zagreb.
Latin - Croatian 454

Žepić, Milan. *Džepni rječnik latinskoga i hrvatskoga jezika za školsku upotrebu.* Vol. I. *Lexicon croatico-latinum.* Vol. II. *Lexicon latino-croaticum.* Zagreb, Hartman, 1902, 450 pp.

94

2 ed: Zagreb, Hartman (St.Kugli), 1913, 371 pp. 13 ed: Zagreb, 1942, 440 pp.
Croatian - Latin
Latin - Croatian 455

Id. *Latinsko-hrvatski (Latinsko-hrvatski ili srpski) rječnik. Lexicon latino-croatico-serbicum.* 3 ed: Zagreb, Školska Knjiga, 1956. 4 ed: Zagreb, ŠK, 1961, 446 pp. 5 ed: Zagreb, ŠK, 1967, 452 pp. 6 ed: Zagreb, ŠK, 1972, 452 pp. 7 ed: Zagreb, ŠK, 1978, 328 pp.
Latin - Croatian 456

Žepić, Sebastijan; Mate Valjavec et al. *Latinsko-hrvatski rječnik za škole.* Zagreb, Naklada Kr. hrvat.-slavon.-dalmat. zemaljske vlade, 1881, VI+1063 pp, in two columns.
Latin - Croatian 457

Special

Doroghy, Zvonimir. *Blago latinskog jezika (Thesaurus linguae latinae).* Zagreb, Matica hrvatska, 1966, 513 pp.
A collection of Latin gnomic expressions: riddles, proverbs, aphorisms, maxims, and other wise sayings 458

Doroghy, Zvonimir; Dinko Chudoba. *Thesaurus linguae latinae.* Zagreb, Tiskara C. Albrecht (P. Acinger), 1933, 232 pp. 459

Jambrešić, Andrija. *Syllabus vocabulorum grammaticae in illyricum sive Croatis et Sclavonibus vernaculam conversorum cum appendice generum declinationum Emanuelis Alvari.* Zagreb, 1726 & 1735. 460

Id. *Manuductio ad croaticam orthographiam.* Zagreb, 1732. 461

Karnarutić (Zadranin), Barne. *Vazetje Sigeta grada.* Zagreb, Narodna Tiskarnica, 1866, LXI+78 pp. Contains: *Hrvatsko-latinski tumač gdjekojih riečih i osobitih izrekah*, pp. 51-78.
Croatian - Latin 462

Katančić, Petar. *In veterem Croatorum patriam indagatio philologica.* Zagreb, Typis Kotscheanis, 1790, 8+52 pp. 463

Kostrenčić, Marko. *Rječnik srednjovjekovne latinštine,* (A - Districtualis). Zagreb, JAZU, 1937. 464

Kostrenčić, Marko et al. *Lexicon latinitatis medii aevi Iugoslaviae.* Zagrabia, Academia Scientiarum et Artium Slavorum Meridionalium, 1969 - . Vol. 1: A - For, XXI+472 pp. Vol. 2: L - Z, 1978, 635-1362 pp.
Latin - Croatian 465

Ladan, Tomislav. *Rječnik nazivaka.* (Latinsko-hrvatski, hrvatskolatinski). In: Frane Petrić, *Nova sveopća filozofija,* Zagreb, Liber, 1979. 466

Pomey, François; Ivan Galjuf. *Flos latinitatis ex auctorum latinae linguae.* Zagreb, 1747, 1797, 1820, 1834, 319 pp.
Latin - Croatian (Kajkavic) phraseological dictionary 467

Romac, Ante. *Latinske pravne izreke.* Zagreb, Globus, 1982. 468

Schlosser - Klekovski; Josip Kalasancij; Ljudevit Vukotinović. *Syllabus florae croaticae additis descriptionibus specium novarum.* Zagrabia, Typis dr. Ludovici Gaj, 1857, V+192+ XVI pp. Contains Croatian botanical terminology.
Croatian - Latin 469

Šugar, Ivan. *Latinsko-hrvatski i hrvatsko-latinski botanički rječnik.* Zagreb, Liber, 1977, 258 pp.
Latin - Croatian
Croatian-Latin 470

Vidović, Radovan. *Pomorski rječnik slavenske obale Jadrana.* Split, Logos, 1984, 590 pp. The second part (pp. 511-540) contains 350 Latin head words. 471

Wagner, F. *Syntaxis ornata.* Zagreb, 1747.
Latin - Croatian (phraseological dictionary) 472

MACEDONIAN

Special

Spektroskopski rječnik. Kemija u industriji. Zagreb, 1982.   473
Croatian - Macedonian

POLISH

Benešić, Julije. *Gramatyka języka chorwackiego czyli serbskiego.* Warszawa, Instytut wydawniczy "Bibljoteka polska", Zakladna tiskara Narodnih novina w Zagrzebiu, 1937, 849 pp. Contains a Croatian-Polish dictionary *Słownik chorwacko-serbsko-polski*, pp. 417-843, ca. 18000 words.
Croatian - Polish   474

Id. *Hrvatsko-poljski rječnik. Słownik chorwacko-polski.* Zagreb, Nakladni Zavod Hrvatske, 1949, XVI+1314 pp. Contains 66,170 Croatian words.
Croatian - Polish   475

Burić, Didak. *Hrvatsko-srpsko-poljski rječnik. Słownik chorwacko-serbsko-polski.* Miejsce Piastowe, Nakl. Tow. Świętego Michała Archanioła, 1935, 469 pp.
Croatian - Polish   476

Frančić, Vilim. *Słownik serbo-chorvacko-polski.* Warszawa, Wiedza Powszechna, 1956-59. Vol. 1: A-M, XXI+828 pp. Vol. 2: N-Ž, VII+1322 pp.
Serbo-Croatian - Polish   477

Ivšić, Stjepan. *Poljsko-hrvatski rječnik.* Ca. 1908, 746+6 leaves. Manuscript is preserved in Zagreb University Library (R 4884)
Polish - Croatian   478

97

RUSSIAN

Finci, Mišo. *Rječnik za osnovne škole. Russko-serbskokhorvatski, srpskohrvatsko-ruski.* Sarajevo, Svjetlost, 1966, 145 pp.
Russian - Serbo-Croatian 479
Serbo-Croatian - Russian

Golik, Miroslav; Aleksandra Golik. *Džepni rusko-hrvatski rječnik.* Zagreb, Velzek, 1946, 295 pp.
Russian - Croatian 480

Grigor'yeva, Radmila Ivanovna. *Kratki serbskokhorvatsko-russki slovar'.* Moskva, GIS, 1960, 640 pp. Ca. 24,000 words.
Serbo-Croatian - Russian 481

Ivanović, S.D. *Karmannyi russko-serbskokhorvatski slovar'.* Moskva, GIS, 1960, 436 pp. Ca. 8,200 words. 2 ed: Moskva, GIS, 1961, 436 pp.
Russian - Serbo-Croatian 482

Ivanović, Slobodan; Josip Petranović. *Russko-serbskokhorvatski slovar'.* Moskva Sovetskaya Entziklopediya, 1965, 784 pp. Ca. 38,000 words. 3 ed: Moskva, SE, 1966, 784 pp. 4 ed: Moskva, SE, 1967, 784 pp. 5 ed: Moskva, 1981. Ca. 40,000 words.
Russian - Serbo-Croatian 483

Ivšić, Stjepan. *Rusko-hrvatski diferencijalni rječnik.* 1947, 5398 leaves. Manuscript preserved in Zagreb University Library (R 4883).
Russian - Croatian 484

Mali rječnik rusko-hrvatski i hrvatsko-ruski. Zagreb, 1922.
Russian - Croatian
Croatian - Russian 485

Menac, Antica et al. *Russko-Horvatskij ili Serbskij Frazeo-logičeskij slovar — Rusko-hrvatski ili sprski frazeološki rječnik.*
Zagreb, Školska Knjiga, 1981, 2 vols., 1537 pp.
Russian - Croatian (phraseological dictionary)
80,000 entries and 35,000 phraseological units   486

Miljković, Tatjana. *Rusko-hrvatski i hrvatsko-ruski džepni rječnik za osnovnu školu.* Zagreb, Školska Knjiga, 1971, 428 pp. 2 ed: 1973, 420 pp. 3 ed: 1975, 428 pp. 4 ed: 1976, 428 pp.
Russian - Croatian
Croatian - Russian   487

Poljanec, F. Radoslav; Serafina M. Madatova-Poljanec. *Russko-horvatskij slovar' — Rusko-hrvatski rječnik.* Zagreb, Školska Knjiga, 1962, XII+996 pp. 2 enl. rev. ed: 1966, XII+ 1180 pp. 3 enl. rev. ed: 1973, XVI+1380 pp.
Russian - Croatian   488

Suvorov, A. *Kratkij horvatsko-russki slovar'.* Zagreb, 1894.
Croatian - Russian   489

Tolstoĭ, Il'ya Il'ich. *Serbsko-khorvatsko-russki slovar'. Srbsko-hrvatsko-ruski rječnik.* Moskva, GIS, 1957, 1168 pp. Ca. 50,000 words. 4 ed. 1976.
Serbo-Croatian - Russian   490

Special

Koračin, Danira. *Tekhnicheski russko-khorvatskoserbski slovar' — minimum.* Zagreb, Radničko Sveučilište 'Moša Pijade', 1967, V+91 pp.
Russian - Croatian   491

Kozicki, Aleksandar. *Rusko-hrvatskosrpski rječnik terminologije vanjske trgovine. Russko-khorvatskoserbski slovar' terminologii vneshneĭ torgovli.* Osijek, Ekonomski Fakultet, 1969, 364 pp.
Russian - Croatian   492

Prohorova Švob, Lenjina.*Rječnik marketinga. Hrvatsko-ruski.* Terminološka Banka Ruske sekcije br. 1. Prilog prevoditelju, broj 11-12, Zagreb, 1979, 30 pp.
   Croatian - Russian   493

SERBIAN

Benešić, Julije. *Gramatyka jezyka chorwatskiego czyli serbskiego.* Warszawa, Instytut wydawniczy 'Bibljoteka polska', Zakladna tiskara Narodnih novina w Zagrzebiu, 1937. 849 pp.
   Contains a differential Serbian-Croatian dictionary, pp. 233-278   494

Guberina, Petar; Kruno Krstić. *Razlike između hrvatskoga i srpskoga književnog jezika.* Zagreb, Matica hrvatska, 1940, 217 pp. Reprinted in Mainz, 1977.
   Contains a differential Serbian-Croatian dictionary pp. 89-217)   495

Tutavac-Bilić, Pero. *Hrvatski jezik nad ponorom.* Buenos Aires, 1963, 139 pp.
   Contains a differential Serbian-Croatian dictionary (pp. 35-135)   496

SLOVAK

Andrić, Josip. *Slovačko-hrvatski rječnik.* Zagreb, 1943.
   Slovak - Croatian   497

SLOVENIAN

Dalmatin, Juraj. *Pentateuh.* Ljubljana, 1578.
   Contains an annexed differential Slovenian - Croatian dictionary comprising 206 Slovenian words and 345 Croatian   498

Id. *Biblija.* Wittenberg, 1584
Contains an annexed differential Slovenian-Croatian
dictionary comprising 761 Slovenian words and 998
Croatian   499

Groebming, Adolf; Ivan Lesica; Vojeslav Molé. *Srpskohrvatsko-*
slovenski slovar. Ljubljana, 1927, 432 pp.
Serbo-Croatian - Slovenian   500

Jurančić, Janko. *Srbohrvatsko-slovenski slovar.* Ljubljana,
Državna založba Slovenije, 1955, XXX+1192 pp. 2 enl. ed.
1972, XXX+1350 pp, ca. 45,000 words
Serbo-Croatian - Slovenian   501

Id. *Srbskohrvatsko-slovenski in slovensko-hrvatsko-srbski*
slovar. Srpskohrvatsko-slovenski i slovensko-srpskohrvatski
rječnik. Ljubljana, Cankarjeva založba, 1970, 566 pp.
Serbo-Croatian - Slovenian
Slovenian - Serbo-Croatian   502

Id. *Slovensko-srpskohrvatski slovar.* Ljubljana, Državna
založba Slovenije, 1981.   503

Koprinski, Robert. *Slovensko-hrvatski slovar.* Ljubljana, Uči-
teljska tiskarna, 1907, XIII+55 pp.
Slovenian - Croatian   504

Musić, August. *Rječnik hrvatsko-slovenski.* Zagreb, Matica
hrvatska, 1887, XVII+66. 2 rev. ed: Zagreb, Matica hrvatska,
1895, XVII+68 pp. 3 ed: 1919, XVI+68 pp. 4 ed. 1925, XVIII+
69 pp.
Croatian - Slovenian   505

Slovensko-hrvatski slovar. Ljubljana, Matica slovenska, 1907,
XIII+55 pp.
Slovenian - Croatian   506

Vilhar, Albin. *Slovensko-srbohrvatski in srbohrvatsko-slovenski rječnik. Slovensko-srbskohrvaški in srbskohrvaško-slovenski slovar.* Ljubljana, Jugoslavenska knjigarna, 1927, 289, 328 pp.
Slovenian - Serbo-Croatian
Serbo-Croatian - Slovenian   507

SPANISH

Velikanović, Iso. *Španjolsko-hrvatski priručni rječnik (diccionario español-croata).* Zagreb, St. Kugli, 1928, 242 pp.
Spanish - Croatian   508

Id. *Hrvatsko-španjolski priručni rječnik.* Zagreb, St. Kugli, 1929, 343+XLI pp.
Croatian - Spanish   509

Id. *Hrvatsko-španjolski i španjolsko-hrvatski rječnik.* Zagreb, 1936, 2 vols.
Croatian - Spanish
Spanish - Croatian   510

Vinja, Vojmir; Ratibor Musanić. *Španjolsko-hrvatskosrpski rječnik. Diccionario español-croataservio.* Zagreb, Školska knjiga, 1971, XVI+1132 pp.
Spanish - Croatian   511

Vinja, Vojmir; Rudolf Kožijan. *Langenscheidtov Univerzalni Rječnik. Španjolsko-hrvatski; Hrvatsko-španjolski.* Zagreb, Mladost, 1972, 527 pp. Other ed. 1978.
Spanish - Croatian
Croatian - Spanish   511a

SWEDISH

Svensk-kroatiskt lexicon. Stockholm, 1985, 568+64 pp. Published by Skolöverstyrelsen — Statens Institut för Läromedels-information.
Swedish - Croatian

TURKISH

Aguşi, Kurteş. *Hrvatskosrpsko-turski i tursko-hrvatskosrpski rječnik.* Istanbul, 1980. Contains 23,389 entries.
Croatian - Turkish
Turkish - Croatian

Kalender, A. *Mali tursko-bosanski rječnik.* Monastir, 1912.
Turkish - Croatian (Bosnian)

Uskufi, Muhamed Heváji. *Makbûli-'Arif.* 1631. Preserved in manuscript. Alija Nametak published an annotated edition of this dictionary in 1968.
Croatian - Turkish dictionary in verses

Special

Blau, Otto. *Bosnisch-türkische Sprachdenkmäler.* Leipzig, 1868.
Turkish loanwords in Bosnia

Esih, Ivan. *Turcizmi — Rječnik turskih, arapskih i perzijskih riječi u hrvatskom književnom jeziku i pučkom govoru.* Zagreb, Vlastita naklada, 1942, 136 pp.
Turkish, Arabic and Persian loanwords in Croatian

Knežević, Anton. *Die Turcismen in der Sprache der Kroaten und Serben.* Münster, Universität, 1962, VII+506 pp.
Turkish loanwords in Croatian and Serbian

UKRAINIAN

VOLAPÜK—SPELIN

Bauer, Juraj. *Spelin-Wörterbuch (Vodobuk spelinir)*. Zagreb,
Leopold Hartman's Buchhandlung, 1892. 43+1 pp.
Contains Volapük dictionary, pp 3-22   526

B L A G O

JEƷIKA SLOVINSKOGA

I L L I

S L O V N I K

ù Koinu ɩsgorarajuſe rjeci slovinſke
Latiniski, ɩ Diacki.

THESAVRuS LINGVAE ILLYRICAE

S I V E

DICTIONARIUM
ILLYRICUM.

In quo verba Illyrica Italicè, & Latinè redduntur.

Labore P. ɪACOBI MICALIA
Societ. JESU collectum.

*Et ſumptibus Sacræ Congregationis
de Propaganda Fide impreſſum*

L A V R E T I,

Apud Paulum, & Io. Baptiſtam Seraphinum. 1649.
Cum DD. Superiorum Permiſsu.

The titlepage of Mikalja's *Blago* . . . (Loreto 1649)

POLYGLOT DICTIONARIES

GENERAL

Bencsics, Nikolaus et al. *Deutsch-Burgenländischkroatisch - Kroatisches Wörterbuch.* Eisenstadt - Zagreb, Edition Roetzer, 1982, 637 pp.
German - Burgenland Croatian - Croatian   527

Capitol's Concise Dictionary. English-Swedish-Dutch-German-French-Italian-Spanish-Croatian. Zagreb, Spektar, 1983, 1188pp. 528

Della Bella, Ardelio. *Dizionario italiano-latino-illirico.* Venezia, 1728, 50+785+177 pp. 2 ed: Dubrovnik, 1785, Vol. 1 (A-H), LVI+395, Vol 2. (J-Z) 448 pp.
Italian - Latin - Croatian   529

Drobnić, Josef. *Ilirsko-němačko-talijanski mali rječnik. Illyrisch-deutsch-italienisches Taschenwörterbuch.* Beč, Tiskom Jermenskoga Monastira, 1846-49, XVIII+530 pp.
Croatian - German - Italian   530

Gelenius, Sigismundus. *Lexicon symphonum quatuor linguarum, Graec. Lat. Germ. ac Sclavinicae.* Basilea, 1537, 55 pp.
Latin, Ancient Greek, German, Czech-Croatian   531

Grgur de, Vitalibus. *Dictionarium trium nobilissimarum Europae linguarum, latinae, illyricae et italicae.* Romae, 1628, 2 vols.
Latin - Croatian - Italian   532

Jambrešić, Andrija; Franjo Sušnik. *Lexicon latinum interpretatione Illyrica, Germanica et Hungarica locuples.* Zagrabiae, Wesseli, 1742, 1068 pp. *Index illyrico sive croatico-latinus* (92 pp.)

Latin - Crotian, German, Hungarian 533

Jurin, Josip. *Calepinus trium linguarum.* (Vol. 1: *Latinsko-hrvatsko-talijanski.* Vol. 2: *Talijansko- latinsko-hrvatski*). In: Rad 315, JAZU. Ca. 1765-73. Manuscript is kept in the library of the Franciscan monastery in Šibenik.

Latin - Croatian - Italian 534

Knapski, Grzegorz. *Thesaurus polono-latino-graecus, seu promptuarium linguae Latinae & Graecae, Polonorum, Roxolanorum, Sclavonum, Boëmorum usui accomodatum.* Cracovia, 1621-25. Other eds: 1632, 2 vols. Posnania, 1698; 1643, 2 vols. Varsovia, 1778-80; 1652, 2 vols; 1686, 2 vols.

Polish - Latin, Ancient Greek, (Ukrainian, Czech, Croatian) 535

Kraljić, I. *Slovnik slavenskij, latinskij, horvatskij.* 1754. Preserved in manuscript. (Island of Krk)

Slavonic - Latin - Croatian 535a

Křižek, Věceslav. *Latinsko-německo-hervatski rěčnik za dolnje gimnazije.* Beč, C. i K. Naklada školskih knjigah, 1862, 1 leaf + 372 pp.

Latin - German - Croatian 536

Leskovar, Ema; Krunoslav Pranjić. *Priručni rječnik (hrvatsko-srpski - engleski - njemački - francuski - talijanski - ruski).* Zagreb, Jugoton, 1965, Part 1 24 pp., 2 ed. 1972, Part 1 24 pp. Part 2 IV+80 pp.

Croatian, English, German, French, Italian, Russian 537

Lodereckerus, Petrus. *Dictionarium septem diversarum linguarum, videlicet Latinae, Italicae, Dalmaticae, Bohemicae, Polonicae & Ungaricae, una cum cujuslibet linguae Registro sive Repertorio.* Pragae, Typographeo Ottmariano, 1605.

Czech, Croatian, German, Hungarian, Italian, Latin, Polish 538

Lux, Sebastian. *Europa in 23 Sprachen, 1000 Wörter bildhaft dargestellt*. München, Deutsche Akademie, 1943, XVI+ 231 pp., illustr. Other ed has the title: *Europa versteht sich.* München, Deutsche Akademie, 1946.

German, Bulgarian, Croatian, Czech, Danish, Dutch, English, Finnish, French, Greek (Modern), Hungarian, Italian, Norwegian, Polish, Portuguese, Rumanian, Russian, Serbian, Slovak, Spanish, Swedish, Turkish, Ukrainian 539

Matijašević, Ivan Marija. *Dizionaretto italiano-slavo-moscovitico*. Dubrovnik, 1751 (A-S). Manuscript is kept in the Zagreb University Library

Italian - Croatian, Russian 540

Megiser, Hieronymus. *Dictionarium quattuor linguarum, videlicet Germanicae, Latinae, Illyricae (quae vulgo slavonica appelatur) et Italicae sive Hetruscae*. Graecii Styriae, 1592. Frankfurt, 1608. 9 ed: Klagenfurt, Kleinmayer, 1744, 392 pp.

German, Latin, Slovenian-Croatian, Italian 541

Micaglia, Jacobus. *Thesaurus linguae illyricae sive Dictionarium Illyricum in quo verba Illyrica Italice et Latine redduntur . . . Blago jezika slovinskoga ili slovnik u komu izgovaraju se rječi slovinske latinski i diački*. Lauratium, Serafini, 1969-51, 13, 46, 863 pp.

Croatian - Italian, Latin 542

Osmojezični enciklopedijski rječnik. Zagreb, Leksikografski zavod, 6 vols. 6000 pp. (In progress). Chief ed. Tomislav Ladan.

Croatian, Russian, English, German, French, Italian, Spanish, Latin 542a

Ouseg, H.L. *International Dictionary in 21 Languages*. New York, Philosophical Library, 1962, XXXI+333 pp.

English, Czech, Danish, Dutch, Finnish, French, German, Hungarian, Italian, Croatian, Norwegian, Polish, Portuguese, Rumanian, Slovak, Spanish, Swedish, Turkish, Russian, Serbian, Ukrainian 543

Palerne, Jean. *Pérégrinations*. Lyon, 1606
Contains a French-Italian-Greek-Turkish-Arabic-Croatian
list of words 544

Pallas, Peter Simon. *Linguarum totius orbis vocabularia
comparativa.* St. Petersburg, 1787-89, 3 vols. 2 ed: Sravni-
tel'nyje slovari vseh' jazikov' i narěčij . . . St. Petersburg,
1787-91, 4 vols.
Croatian Kajkavic and *i*-Štokavic words figure in this
dictionary known as *Vocabularium Catharinae* 545

Patačić, Adam. *Dictionarium Latino-Illyricum et Germanicum.
Pulcherrimo rerum ac materiarum Ordine ad diversas Classes
digestum, vocabulorum ad quamvis materiam, scientiam,
artem et vitae humanae usum pertinentium ubertate insigne.
Proloquiis, notis et eruditis animadversionibus refertum,
concinnavit.* Ca. 1772-79, XIII+V+1054 + index 48 pp. Manuscript is kept in the diocesan archives in Kalocza (Hungary)
Latin - Croatian (Kajkavic) - German 546

*Radices latinae linguae cum derivatis et compositis suis in
tribus idiomatibus latino-croatico-germanicis.* Zagreb, 1788;
Budim, 1801 547

*Rječnik srpskohrvatsko-češko-poljski; češko-poljsko-srpsko-
hrvatski i poljsko-srpskohrvatski-češki.* Zagreb, Savez
slavenskih štedionica, 1937, VIII+98+XVI+96+XVI+95
+XX pp.
Croatian - Czech - Polish 548

Rožić, Anton. *Vocabularium iliti Rechnik najpotrebneshe
rechi vu treh jezikih zadersavajuchi.* Varaždin, 1822, 32 pp.
2 ed. 1833, 31 pp.
Latin - Croatian (Kajkavic) - German 549

Stulli (Stulić), Joakim. *Lexicon Latino-Italico-Illyricum . . .
Vocabolario italiano-illirico-latino.* Buda, Universitas Pestana,
1801, 800, 810 pp.
Latin - Italian - Croatian 550

Id. *Rjecsosloxje, illyrico-latino-italicum.* Ragusa, Martecchini, 1806, 727, 674 pp.
Croatian - Italian - Latin 551

Id. *Vocabolario italiano-illirico-latino.* Ragusa, Martecchini, 1810, 838, 862 pp.
Italian - Croatian - Latin 552

Szeged-szótár illyr, magyar és német. Kalocza, 1867
Croatian - Hungarian - German 553

Talijansko-hrvatsko-ruski rječnik. 1751. Printed in: *Zbornik Radova Filozofskog Fakulteta Sveučilišta u Zagrebu,* vol. 1, pp. 567-612, Zagreb, 1951
Italian - Croatian - Russian 554

Tanzlinger-Zanotti, Ivan. *Vocabolario di tre nobilissimi linguaggi, italiano, illirico e latino, con l'aggiunta di molte erbe semplici e termini militari.* Zadar, 1679, 138 leaves. 2 ed: 1704, 1281 pp. 3 ed: 1732, 2 vols. Vol. 2 contains *Indice illirico scelto dal vocabolario suddetto.*
Italian - Croatian - Latin 555

Verantius (Vrančić), Faustus. *Dictionarium quinque nobilissimarum Europae linguarum, Latinae, Italicae, Germanicae, Dalmatiae et Ungaricae cum vocabulis Dalmaticis quae Ungari sibi usurparunt.* Venetia, Moretto, 1595, 128 pp. 2 ed: see Lodereckerus, Petrus. 3 ed: Posonium, Typis Belnayanis, 1834 (ed. Josephus Thewrewk de Ponor)
Reprint: Zagreb, Liber, 1971, 135 pp.
Latin - Italian - German - Croatian - Hungarian 556

Vocabularium trilingue. The 17th c. manuscript kept in Perugia.
Croatian - Italian - Latin 557

Vocabularium trilingue germanico-latino-croaticum. 18th c.,
14 leaves, in 3 cols., manuscript kept in Zagreb University
Library (R 4355)
    German - Latin - Croatian   558

Voltiggi (Voltić), Josip. *Ricsoslovnik illirickskoga, italianskoga
i nimacskoga jezika, s jednom pridpostavljenom grammatikom
ili pismenstvom. Illyrisch- italienisch und deutsches Wörterbuch und Grammatik.* Wien, Kurtzbeck, 1803, LIX+610 pp,
ca. 17000 words.
    Croatian - German - Italian   559

SPECIAL

Androić, Mirko et al. *Rječnik arhivske terminologije Jugoslavije.* Zagreb, 1972, X+78 pp.
    Croatian - Serbian - Slovenian - Macedonian - English -
    French - German - Russian - Italian   560

Arambašin, Joso. *Liječnički rječnik.* Split, Hrv. štamparija,
Trumbić i drug, 1912, VII+362 pp.
    Latin - Croatian - German   561

Id. *Prinovljeni liječnički rječnik.* Split, 1940, 327 pp.
    Revised Medical dictionary.   562

Babić, Božo. *Nazivlje korita i jedrila broda u hrvatskom,
njemačkom i talijanskom jeziku.* Kraljevica, Primorska tiskara,
1877, 22 pp.
    Terms for hulls and sailing boats in Croatian, German,
    and Italian   563

Id. *Zapovjed brodovnih obava u hrvatskom, njemačkom i
talijanskom jeziku.* Bakar, Stiglić I. Desselbrunner, 1878, 20 pp.
    Croatian - German - Italian   564

Id. *Pomorski rječnik ili Nazivlje za brodarenje po moru.* Senj,
Ivo Hreljanović, 1901, 59+1 pp.
    Italian - Croatian - German   565

Bajželj, Ivan. *Slovarček sokolskih nazivov, slovenskih, hrvaš-kih, srbskih in čeških.* Ljubljana, Jugoslovanska Sokolska Matica, 1925, 21 pp.
Slovenian, Croatian, Serbian, Czech   566

Beaufort scale. Official designation used in maritime countries 13t of wind force. Monaco, International Hydrographic Bureau, 1931.
Norwegian, Swedish, Finnish, Russian, Estonian, Latvian, Lithuanian, Polish, German, Danish, Icelandic, Dutch, French, Spanish, Portuguese, Italian, Croatian, Greek (Modern), Turkish, Bulgarian, Rumanian, Siamese, Chinese, Japanese, American English, British English, Latin, American Spanish, Brasilian Portuguese   567

Berman, Peter M. *The concise dictionary of 26 languages in simultaneous translations.* New York, Bergman, 1968, 408 pp.
English, French, Spanish, Italian, Portuguese, Rumanian, German, Dutch, Swedish, Danish, Norwegian, Polish, Czech, Serbo-Croatian, Hungarian, Finnish, Turkish, Indonesian, Swahili, Esperanto, Russian, Greek (Modern), Arabic, Hebrew, Yiddish, Japanese   568

Biraud, Yves. *Lexique polyglotte des maladies contagieuses. Polyglot dictionary of communicable diseases* (League of Nations. Bulletin of the Health Organization, Geneva, vol. 10, 1943-44, pp. 203-556)
French, Bulgarian, Czech, Danish, Dutch, English, Estonian, Finnish, German, Greek (Modern), Hungarian, Icelandic, Italian, Latin, Latvian, Lithuanian, Norwegian, Polish, Portuguese, Rumanian, Russian, Serbo-Croatian, Spanish, Swedish, Turkish
Polyglot index in one alphabet   569

Borčić, Branko. *Višejezični kartografski rječnik.* Zagreb, Geodetski fakultet Sveučilišta u Zagrebu, 1977, 442 pp. 1977
Croatian - English - French - German - Russian   570

Božičević, Juraj. *Automatsko vođenje procesa.* Zagreb, Tehnička Knjiga, 1971. Contains Croatian-English-German-Russian dictionary of automation (pp. 235-262). 570a

Brodska nomenklatura. Rijeka, Pomorstvo, 1951, XV+254 pp.
Shipping nomenclature
Croatian - English - Italian 571

Cowles Pehòtsky, Barbara. *Bibliographer's glossary of foreign words and phrases; an alphabet of terms in bibliographical and booktrade-use compiled from 20 languages.* New York, Bowker, 1935, 82 pp.
Bulgarian, Croatian, Czech, Danish-Norwegian, Dutch, Finnish, French, German, Ancient Greek, Hungarian, Italian, Latin, Lithuanian, Polish, Portuguese, Rumanian, Russian, Serbian, Spanish, Swedish → English 572

Crnić, Rudolf. *Pomorski rječnik (talijansko-njemački-hrvatski).* Zagreb, Jugoslavenski Kompas, 1922, 2+38 pp., in three columns. Ca. 2700 terms
Nautical dictionary, Italian - German - Croatian 573

Čampara, Ešref. *Međunarodni rječnik arhitekture, građevinarstva i urbanizma. Hrvatski ili srpski - francuski - engleski - njemački - ruski.* Zagreb, GZH, 1984.
Croatian - French - English - German - Russian 574

Dabac, Vlatko. *Ilustrirani tehnički rječnik. Na hrvatskom, njemačkom, engleskom, talijanskom i španjolskom jeziku. Elementi strojeva.* Zagreb, Tehnička knjiga, 1951.
Croatian - German - English - Italian - Spanish 575

Delcambre, Emile Emmanuel; Rollet de l'Isle. *Lexique météorologique.* Paris, Office Nationale Météorologique de France, 1931, 429 pp.
French - Croatian, Czech, English, Esperanto, German, Italian, Polish, Portuguese, Rumanian, Russian, Spanish 575a

114

Deželić, Mladen. *Građa za kemijski rječnik (hrvatsko-njemačko-talijansko-englezki)*. Zagreb, 1942, 27 pp.
Croatian - German - Italian - English   576

Dictionarium bibliothecari practicum. Wiesbaden, Harrasowitz, 1968
Bulgarian, Croatian, Czech, Danish, Dutch, English, Finnish, French, German, Greek (Modern), Hungarian, Italian, Latin, Polish, Rumanian, Russian, Serbian, Slovenian, Spanish, Swedish   577

Dolenský, Evžen. *Šestijazyčný plýnarenský slovník. The gas industry vocabulary. Plinarski rječnik. Slownik gazowniczy.* Praha, Plynárenské, Vodárenské a Zdravotně-Technické Sdružení, 1939, 384 pp.
Czech, English, French, German, Polish, Croatian   578

Dreizehnsprachiges Wörterbuch für Gebirgsmechanik. Berlin, Akademie, 1970, 487 pp.
German - Bulgarian, Czech, English, French, Hungarian, Polish, Portuguese, Rumanian, Russian, Serbo-Croatian, Spanish, Swedish   579

Fischer, H.F.; F. Linka. *Obućarski rječnik.* Zagreb, Trgovinska komora NR Hrvatske, 1960, 124 pp.
Croatian - English, French, German   580

Glossary of cartographic terms and manual of symbols and abbreviations used on the navigational charts of the various countries. 3 ed: Monaco, International Hydrographic Bureau, 1951, XV+188 pp. Suppl: 1956, 36 pp.
English and French with Chinese, Danish, Dutch, German, Greek (Modern), Italian, Croatian, Japanese, Norwegian, Polish, Portuguese, Russian, Siamese, Spanish, Swedish equivalents   581

Glossary of selected map terms relative to authorities, dates, scales, editions, and locations in foreign text maps. Washington, U.S. Army Map Service, 1944, 47 leaves

Bulgarian, Chinese, Czech, Danish, Dutch, Finnish, French, German, Hungarian, Italian, Japanese, Norwegian, Polish, Portuguese, Rumanian, Russian, Serbo-Croatian, Siamese, Spanish, Swedish 582

Hadžiomeragić, M. *Rječnik stomatologije.* Zagreb, Vlastita naklada, 1978.

English - German - Croatian 583

Hirtz, Miroslav. *Rječnik peradarstva.* Beograd, Državna štamparija, 1934, 238 pp.

Croatian - German - Latin 584

Holt, S.J. *Multilingual vocabulary and notation for fishery dynamics. Vocabulaire multilingue et notation pour la dynamique des pêches.* Rome, F.A.O., 1960, 72 pp.

Afrikaans, Croatian, Danish, Dutch, English, Estonian, Finnish, French, German, Icelandic, Indonesian, Italian, Japanese, Malayan, Norwegian, Polish, Portuguese, Russian, Slovenian, Spanish, Swedish 585

Ilustrirani tehnički rječnik; hrvatsko - njemačko - englesko - francusko - talijansko - španjolsko - ruski, elementi strojeva. Illustriertes technisches Wörterbuch;Maschinenelemente. Machine elements. Zagreb, Tehnička Knjiga, 1952, XXIII+ 534 pp.

Croatian, German, English, French, Italian, Spanish, Russian 586

International illustrated dictionary of mechanical handling. 96 terms, London, Mechanical Handling Engineers Assn., 1950, 39 pp. ill. 5 ed: London, 1958, 48 pp., 143 terms

Croatian, English, French, German, Italian, Spanish 587

Keresztesy, Sándor. *Idegen nyelvek szótára. Tájékoztató a német, francia, olasz, lengyel, horvát, angol, szerb, cseh és román nyelvü átiratok megértéséhez.* Budapest, 1910.
German, French, Italian, Polish, Croatian, English, Serbian, Czech, Rumanian   588

Jal, A. *Glossaire nautique; repertoire polyglotte de termes de marine anciens et modernes.* Paris, Didot, 1848-50, 1591 pp.
Contains some Russian and a few hundred Croatian terms. Croatian terms are reprinted in: Luetić, Josip, *Naša pomorska terminologija u A. Jal-ovom »Glossaire nautique« iz 1848 g.* (Ljetopis Jugoslavenske Akademije, Knjiga 61, pp. 248-254, Zagreb, 1956)   589

Jørgensen, Harriet, Ingeborg. *Nomina avium europearum.* Copenhagen, Munksgaard, 1958, XII+283 pp., 639 terms
Croatian, Czech, Danish, Dutch, English, Finnish, French, German, Greek (Modern), Hungarian, Icelandic, Italian, Latin, Norwegian, Polish, Portuguese, Russian, Spanish, Swedish, Turkish   590

Jugoslavenska tehnička terminologija, prilog 'Tehničkog lista', Zagreb, 15 Nov. 1920 - June 1922, 19 fascicles, 216 pp., 8500 terms
Technical terminology
German - Croatian - Serbian - Slovenian   591

Juridisch-politische Terminologie für die slavischen Sprachen Oesterreichs; Deutsch-kroatische, serbische und slovenische Separatausgabe. Wien, Hof- und Staatsdruckerei, 1853, XIV+694 pp.
German - Croatian, Serbian, Slovenian   592

Kahane, Henry; Renée Kahane; Olga Koshansky. *Venetian nautical terms in Dalmatia.* (Romance Philology, Vol. 7, 1953-54, pp. 156-170, 333-342)
Contains a word list
English, Italian, Croatian   593

117

Ladan, Tomislav. *Grčko-latinsko-hrvatski rječnik temeljnih pojmova ili nazivaka.* In *Nikomahova etika,* Zagreb, Liber, 1982, 350 pp.

Greek - Latin - Croatian   594

Maver, Giovanni. *Parole serbocroate o slovene di origine italiana (dalmatica).* (Slavia, vol. 2, pp. 32-43) Praha, 1923-24.

Serbo-Croatian, Slovenian, Italian   595

Mentzel, Christian. *Pinax Botanorymos Polyglottos Index nominum plantarum universalis.* Berlin, Daniel Reichelius, 1682, 331 pp. Other eds: 1696, *Lexicon plantarum polyglotton universale.* Berlin, C.G. Nicolai, 1715

Latin, Greek (Ancient), Italian, Spanish, Portuguese, French, English, Danish, German, N, Czech, Polish, Lithuanian, Hungarian, Slovenian, Croatian, Hebrew, Aramaic, Syriac, Arabic, Turkish, Persian, Malabar, Hindi, Cingalese, Javanese, Chinese, Japanese, Malayan, Korean and dialects   596

Mlakar, France; Vladimir Muljević. *Šestjezični rječnik s područja regulacije i automacije.* Zbornik radova *Jurema* (1964) No 1, pp. 441-471

Automation glossary

Croatian - Slovenian - English - German - French - Italian   597

Móra, Imre. *The Publisher's Practical Dictionary in 20 Languages.* München-Pullach, Verlag Dokumentation, 1974, 389 pp. 2 ed: München, 1977, 389 pp.

German, English, French, Russian, Spanish, Bulgarian, Finnish, Dutch, Italian, Croatian, Norwegian, Polish, Portuguese, Rumanian, Swedish, Serbian, Slovak, Czech, Hungarian   598

118

Morskoj atlas. Kratkij slovar morskih geografičeskih terminov.
Vol 1: *Ukazatel' geografičeskih nazvanij*, pp. 493-539. Moskva,
Voennomorskoe ministerstvo Sojuza SSR, 1952
Albanian, Arabic, Bulgarian, Chinese, Croatian, Danish,
Dutch, English, Finnish, French, German, Greek
(Modern), Hindi, Italian, Japanese, Korean, Malayan,
Norwegian, Persian, Polish, Portuguese, Rumanian,
Russian, Spanish, Swedish, Turkish   599

Multilingual collection of terms for welding and allied proces-
ses. Resistance welding, gas welding, arc welding, general
terms. Basle, International Institute of Welding, 1955-1961,
253, 24, 132, 140, 27 pp.
English, Croatian, Czech, Danish, Dutch, Finnish, French,
German, Italian, Norwegian, Polish, Portuguese, Russian,
Slovak, Slovenian, Spanish, Swedish, Turkish   600

Muljević, Vladimir; et al. *Klimatizacija i rashladna tehnika.*
Englesko-njemačko-francusko-rusko-hrvatski. Zagreb, Tehnička
knjiga, 1983, 300 pp.
English - German - French - Russian - Croatian   601

Id. *Obrada podataka i programiranje. Englesko-njemačko-*
francusko-rusko-hrvatski. Zagreb, Tehnička knjiga, 1984, 360 pp.
English - German - French - Russian - Croatian   602

Id. *Automatizacija. Englesko-njemačko-francusko-rusko-hrvat-*
ski. Zagreb, Tehnička knjiga, 1985, 400 pp.
English - German - French - Russian - Croatian   603

Id. *Medicin-tehnika. Englesko-njemačko-francusko-rusko-hrvat-*
ski. Zagreb, Tehnička knjiga, 1985, 400 pp.
English - German - French - Russian - Croatian   604

Nemičić, Milan. *Ljekarski rječnik,* I *Njemačko-latinski-hrvatski*
dio. Zagreb, Nakl. Kr. hrv.-slav.-dalm. zemaljske vlade, 1898,
VI+III+998 pp.
Dictionary of medical terms
German - Latin - Croatian   605

Id. *Medicinski rječnik* (*Lexicon medicum*). *Njemačko-latinski-hrvatski*, I-II. Zagreb, Nakl. Kr. hrv.-slav.-dalm. zemaljske vlade, 1913, IX+1242 pp.
Dictionary of medical terms
German - Latin - Croatian 606

Nomenclature et vocabulaire concernant les feux. Nomenclature and vocabulary concerning lights. Monaco, Bureau Hydrographique International, 1946
English, Bulgarian, Danish, Dutch, Estonian, Finnish, French, German, Greek (Modern), Icelandic, Italian, Japanese, Latvian, Norwegian, Portuguese, Russian, Serbo-Croatian, Spanish, Swedish 607

Pinto, Olga. *Termini d'uso nelle Bibliografie dei Periodici.* Roma, Libreria di Scienze e Lettere, 1929, 89 pp.
Latin, Italian, French, Spanish, Portuguese, Rumanian, Esperanto, English, German, N, Danish, Norwegian, Swedish, Russian, Ukrainian, Bulgarian, Serbian, Croatian, Czech, Polish, Albanian, Greek. (Modern), Hungarian, Finnish, Estonian, Lettish, Lithuanian, Turkish, Persian, Arabic, Hebrew, Yiddish, Armenian, Georgian, Thai, Chinese, Japanese 608

Pipics, Zoltán. *A Könyvtáros gyákarlati szótára. Dictionarium bibliothecarii practicum.* Budapest, Gondolat, 1963, 317 pp. Other ed: 1964
Hungarian - English, Bulgarian, Croatian, Czech, Danish, Finnish, French, German, Greek (Modern), Italian, Latin, N, Polish, Rumanian, Russian, Serbian, Slovak, Spanish, Swedish 609

Id. *Dictionarium bibliothecarii practicum. Wörterbuch des Bibliothekars. The Librarian's practical Dictionary. In 20 Languages.* München-Pullach, Verlag Dokumentation, 1969,

375 pp. Other eds: 1970, 1971, 1974, 385 pp.

German - English, Bulgarian, Croatian, Czech, Danish, Finnish, French, Greek (Modern), Hungarian, Italian, Latin, N, Polish, Rumanian, Russian, Serbian, Slovak, Spanish, Swedish 610

Id. *Dictionarium Bibliothecarii Practicum ad usum internationalem, in XXII linguis. The Librarian's Practical Dictionary in 22 languages. Wörterbuch des Bibliothekars in 22 Sprachen.* München-Pullach, Verlag Dokumentation, 1974, 385 pp. Other ed: Budapest, Akadémiai Kiadó, 1977, 385 pp. 7 ed: Verlag Dokumentation, München, 1977

English - Bulgarian, Croatian, Czech, Danish, Finnish, French, German, Greek (Modern), Hungarian, Italian, Latin, N, Polish, Rumanian, Russian, Serbian, Slovak, Spanish, Swedish, Norwegian, Portuguese 611

Preuschen, G.; J. Piel-Des-Ruisseaux et al. *Symbola. Landwirtschaftliche Symbole.* 4 ed: Bad Kreuznach, Max-Planck-Institut für Landarbeit und Landtechnik, 1962, 160 pp.

German - Croatian, Dutch, English, Finnish, French, Hungarian, Italian, Polish, Portuguese, Russian, Serbian, Spanish, Swedish 612

Raić, Lazar. *Formule i upute za ocjenjivanje trofeja.* Zagreb, Lovačka Knjiga, 1959, 169 pp.

Hunting terminology
Croatian - German - French 613

Riječi iz istočnih jezika koje se upotrebljavaju u Bosni i Hercegovini. Sarajevo, Kajon, 1910, 56 pp.

Oriental (Turkish, Arabic, Persian) - Croatian 614

Rječnik automobilskih izraza na hrvatskom, njemačkom, engleskom, francuskom i talijanskom jeziku. Zagreb, Auto-Moto Savez Hrvatske, 1954, 62 pp. 350 terms

Croatian, German, English, French, Italian 615

Roccabonella, Niccolò. *Liber de simplicibus*. Zadar, 1449, 483 pp. + 432 pictures. Manuscript kept in Marciana (Venice)
Botanical dictionary (illustrated)
Arabic - Greek - Latin - Croatian 616

Simeon, Rikard. *Enciklopedijski rječnik lingvističkih naziva na 8 jezika*. 2 vols. Zagreb, Matica hrvatska, 1969, Vol. 1 LXIV + 1010 pp; Vol. 2 XIII + 926 pp.
Encyclopedic Dictionary of Linguistic terms
Croatian, Latin, English, French, German, Italian, Russian, Spanish 617

Smirić, E. *Terminologia ufficiale italiano-serba o croato - tedesca. Italienisch-serbisch oder kroatisch-deutsche Amtsterminologie*. Zagabria, Maravić, 1904, 910 pp.
Italian - Serbian or Croatian - German 618

Id. *Deutsch-italienisch-kroatische oder serbische Amtsterminologie. Njemačko-talijanska-hrvatska ili srpska službena terminologija*. Mali Lošinj, 1911.
German - Italian - Croatian 619

Šegvić, Kerubin. *Trgovački rječnik talijanski, engleski, francuski i njemački. Vocabolario commerciale italiano tradotto in serbo-croato, inglese, francese e tedesco*. Zagreb, Tisak i naklada St. Kugli, 1925, 5-59 pp.
Commercial dictionary
Croatian - Italian - English - French - German 620

Špoljarić, Zvonimir et al. *Višejezični rječnik stručnih izraza u anatomiji drva*. Zagreb, Udruženje Šumarsko Privrednih Organizacija, 1969, 86 pp.
Croatian, English, French, German, Italian, Portuguese, Spanish 621

Šulek, Bogoslav. *Hrvatsko-njemačko-talijanski rječnik znanstvenog nazivlja. Deutsch-kroatische wissenschaftliche Terminologie. Terminologia scientifica italiano-croata*. I-II.

122

Zagreb, Tiskom Narodne tiskare dra Ljudevita Gaja, 1874-75, XXVI + 1372 pp.
Croatian, German, Italian 622

Tableaux des principaux caractères des feux. Monaco, Bureau Hydrographique International, 1937, 1 table
French, German, English, N, Spanish, Italian, Portuguese, Danish, Norwegian, Swedish, Icelandic, Finnish, Estonian, Lettish, Russian, Polish, Bulgarian, Croatian, Greek (Modern), Japanese, Chinese, Thai 623

Tabulation of the terminology of submarine relief. Tableau de la terminologie du relief sous-marin. Monaco, International Hydrographic Bureau, 1932, 1 tab.; Corr. 1, 1938; Corr. 2, 1939
French, English, Spanish, German, Arabic, Croatian, Lettish, Finnish, Bulgarian, Estonian, Italian, Lithuanian, Rumanian, Chinese, Danish, Greek (Modern), Japanese, Portuguese, Swedish, Norwegian, Thai 624

Turk, S. et al. *Obrada podataka i programiranje. Engleski-njemački-francuski-ruski-hrvatski.* Zagreb, Tehnička Knjiga, 1984.
Data and programming terminology
English, German, French, Russian, Croatian 625

Uni. *Nomenclatura delle specie legnose che vegetano spontanee in Italia.* Milano, Ente Nazionale Italiano di Unificazione, 1945, 12 pp.
Italian - Croatian, English, French, German, Spanish 626

Vocabulaire des termes usuels des avis aux navigateurs radiotélégraphiques. Vocabulary of terms commonly used in radio messages for navigators. Monaco, Bureau Hydrographique International 1939, 5 tables.
French, English, Danish, Spanish, Italian, N, Norwegian, Portuguese, Swedish, Finnish, Estonian, Croatian, Japanese, Polish, Greek (Modern), Turkish, Lettish 627

ADMODUM REVERENDI PATRIS

JOANNIS

BELLOSZTÉNËCZ,

E SACRA D. PAULI PRIMI EREMITÆ RELIGIONE

GAZOPHYLACIUM,

SEU

LATINO-ILLYRICORUM ONOMATUM

ÆRARIUM,

SELECTIORIBUS SYNONIMIS,
PHRASEOLOGIIS, VERBORUM CON-
STRUCTIONIBUS METAPHORIS, ADAGIIS,
ABUNDANTISSIME LOCUPLETATUM,

ITEM

PLURIMIS AUTHORUM IN HOC OPERE
ADDUCTORUM SENTENTIIS IDIOMATE ILLY-
RICO DELICATIS ILLUSTRATUM.

Penultimarum duntaxat Syllabarum Quantitatibus, litteris *p.c.* i.e.
penultima correpta, & *p p.* i.e. penultima producta, ubique denotatis,
ifgnatum. Refiduis ex Epitome in Profodiæ fpeciales Regulas, Pantaleonis
Bartolonæi Raverini, in Calce Libri appofito, colligendis

ATQUE HACTENUS INTERCLUSUM.

Et nunc primùm peculiariter Illyriorum commodo
A P E R T U M.

ZAGRABIÆ.

Typis Joannis Baptiftæ Weitz, Inclyti Regni Croatiæ Typographi.
In Anno Domini M.DCC XL.

The titlepage of Belostenec's *Gazophylacium* . . . (Zagreb 1740)

AUTHOR INDEX

Numbers refer to entries, not pages

LANGUAGE INDEX

Numbers refer to entries, not pages

SUBJECT INDEX

Numbers refer to entries, not pages

DIZIONARIO
ITALIANO-LATINO-ILLIRICO

A cui fi premettono alcune brevi Inftruzioni Gramaticali, neceffarie per apprendere la Lingua e l'Ortografia Illirica.

OPERA DEL PADRE
ARDELIO DELLA BELLA
DELLA COMPAGNIA DI GESU'.

PRIMA EDIZIONE RAGUSEA

Ricorretta nell' Ortografia Illirica ed Italiana, e da moltiffimi altri errori emendata; arricchita di termini propri delle Scienze e delle Arti; e di nuove Fraſi, di Proverbj, di Modi di dire; e notabilmente accrefciuta de' nomi di Regni, di Città, di Provincie, di Fiumi, di Monti, di Mari ec. delle Piante, deli' Erbe, de' Fiori ec. degli Animali, degli Uccelli ec. nella prima Edizione mancanti.

TOMO PRIMO
DEDICATO
ALL' ECCELSO SENATO
DELLA REPUBBLICA DI RAGUSA.

RAGUSA MDCCLXXXV.

Nella Stamperia Privilegiata.

Sermage

The titlepage of Della Bella's *Dizionario* . . . (Dubrovnik 1785)

CONTENTS

N° d'éditeur 1191
Dépôt légal. — 4ᵉ trimestre 1985